# Reflective Reading

## Engaging and Practical Ideas for Teaching Reading Comprehension in the Primary Classroom

## Anne Glennie

cranachan

First published in 2017 by Cranachan Publishing Limited
Copyright © Anne Glennie 2017

The moral right of Anne Glennie to be identified as the author of this work has been asserted by her in accordance with the Copyright, Designs and patents Act, 1988.
All rights reserved.
No part of this publication may be reproduced or transmitted in any form by any means, electronic or mechanical, including photocopying, recording or any information storage or retrieval system, without the prior permission of the publisher.

ISBN: 978-1-911279-20-4

*Comprehension Compass Design* by Katie Quinn Illustration
www.oohkatieq.co.uk
Twitter: @oohkatieq
Instagram: @oohkatieq

*Comprehension Compass* Copyright © Anne Glennie

Extracts from *Curriculum for Excellence*, the *Experiences and Outcomes*, the *Literacy and English Principles and Practice* and the *Benchmarks* © Crown Copyright 2017
Reproduced under the terms of the Open Government Licence
http://www.nationalarchives.gov.uk/doc/open-government-licence/version/3/

(see full list of acknowledgements and permissions at the back of this book)

Every effort has been made to trace copyright holders of material reproduced in this book, and the publishers apologise for any inadvertent omissions.

All internet addresses/Twitter handles were valid at the time of going to press. Due to the nature of the web, some details may have changed since publication. While we regret any inconvenience this may cause, no responsibility for any such changes can be accepted by either the author or the publisher. We strongly recommend that teachers check websites before using them in the classroom.

Cover Design and Typesetting by Cranachan Publishing

Extra bits by Jeffrey the Giraffe

www.cranachanpublishing.co.uk

@cranachanbooks

for Mrs Clarke

# FEEDBACK FROM THE CHALKFACE ABOUT REFLECTIVE READING

The single best course I have thus far attended in 21 years of teaching. This is why I came into the job.
*Mark Woods, Class Teacher*

Thank you very much for today. I feel this will make a huge impact on my practice. I would be delighted to have more of our teachers trained.
*Barry Donaldson, Literacy Support Officer*

An outstanding delivery of an extremely informative course. Everybody needs to sign up for this course ASAP!
*Maggie McEntee, Class Teacher*

Anne struck a perfect balance of entertainment, content, theory and practical activities!
*Andrine Black, Class Teacher (ASN-SEBN)*

Thank you for the best-ever Inset day! Friend for life :D
*Wendy Rennie, Class Teacher*

Anne is so inspiring and easy to listen to. Today has whizzed by because she is engaging, energetic and creative. Anne has personally helped me to feel re-energised and I am now very keen to change things and to try out her ideas and make reading better in my classroom!
*Lucy Power, Class Teacher*

Excellent course, Anne. Great to see it at the leading edge of current research. Thank you for all the support that you've provided our Authority.
*James Cook, Literacy and Assessment Development Officer*

I thought this was a very useful course backed by research and tailor-made to suit CfE. Thanks to Anne for an inspirational day.
*Kirsty Greenwood, Class Teacher*

What a fantastic day! Love the ideas to help share a love of reading. Reading is my passion so anything that gives me an opportunity to share strategies to use is a bonus. Thanks for a great, useful day.
*Tracey Michie, Depute Head*

This has taken me way longer than I meant it to, but I just wanted to thank you so, SO much for the course last Wednesday. I can honestly say that it was the single best CPD training I have attended in my career and I came away feeling really excited.
*Kate McJennett, Secondary English Teacher*

Really enjoyed it. The speaker (Anne) was engaging and inspiring. I've been given lots practical things to action and a lot of food for thought. An incredible resource—thank you very much.
*Jessica Pollock, Class Teacher*

Very useful resources. Really engaging & motivating presentation. Thanks Anne—you have inspired and rejuvenated me!
*Janey Nicol, Class Teacher*

A fantastic course which has got me excited about reading with my class. Excellent resources which are tailored to the children. I can't wait to get planning. Excellent presenting skills! Thank you!! :D
*Stephanie Young, Class Teacher*

Very interesting and relevant for my needs and the needs of the school. Very inspiring.
*Debbie Mercer, DHT*

Anne is an excellent presenter and inspiring. I did this course in June and have been implementing the strategies since. My class love it, as do I!
*Rachael Quinn, Class Teacher*

Very educational and inspiring. I will use the materials and tweet the outcome. Thank you.
*Michelle Hoppé, Class Teacher*

Reflective Reading is simply a methodology. However, it is a rather marvellous one. You, Anne, are doing excellent things... this good practice really needs a wider audience. It would ensure consistency of approach and quality across Scotland, not just the pockets/people who can afford to attend this training.
*Iain Morrow, Principal Teacher*

# Contents

## Introduction

## 1 You Are What You Read

## 2 How to Build a Reader

## 3 Planning, Tracking and Assessment

# 4 Teaching and Learning: Short Read

# 5 Teaching and Learning: Long Read

# 6 Managing Reading in the Classroom

# Appendix

*LOOK* Supporting lesson plans, activities, and resources to get you started can be downloaded here—or use the QR code—fancy!

**www.thelearningzoo.co.uk/bookstuff**

# Read.

# LEARN.

# Sleep.

# Repeat.

# Introduction

Today, children are exposed to more text, information and language than ever before. From games to graphic novels, social media and films, to the whole of the internet and ever-present advertising—children's lives are filled with opportunities to read. Technology is changing, not just how we access our information, but the way in which we interact with it. Reading is no longer only about books; it is everything you read, watch or listen to.

Whether your device of choice is a phone or laptop, whether you're glued to a tablet or a television (or perhaps both at the same time), or whether you're having an analogue moment and are tucked up in bed with a good, old-fashioned book, we are constantly bombarded by ideas, opinions and stories. We need to teach children how to be effective readers in this text-laden environment—to discover how a text affects or entertains them, to understand how it informs or persuades them, to consider how it challenges their ideas, or attempts to influence their thinking.

Reflective Reading aims to unlock the magic of being a reader who understands, enjoys and appreciates what they read, regardless of the form it takes; a reader who is confident, critical and capable of translating words, sounds and pictures into meaning. A reader who is not only ready for the rest of the 21st century, but one who is also capable of accessing and understanding 'the best which has been thought and said' from our past.

This book contains everything you need to start using the Reflective Reading methodology in your school, wherever you are in the world. Each chapter deals with a different aspect of reading practice and often includes 'homework' or sample lessons to support implementation in the classroom. In this way, you can reflect on the chapter's content and try out some of the ideas and activities, to see how it works for you and your class. Further reading suggestions are also given for those of you who wish to do more background reading on each subject.

We hope you enjoy putting reading 'back on the map' and making reading at school magic.

Are you sitting comfortably? Then let's begin...

*Anne & Jeffrey x*

**Anne Glennie &
Jeffrey the Giraffe**

**The Learning Zoo HQ**

**@anneglennie**

#staycurious

# CHAPTER 1

# You Are What You Read

# CHAPTER 1
# You Are What You Read

## WHAT IS REFLECTIVE READING?

Originally written to support teachers implementing the new and innovative Scottish curriculum, (*Curriculum for Excellence*), *Reflective Reading* is a methodology that can be used wherever reading and comprehension requires to be taught. While the concept originated in my primary classroom, the materials have found their way into secondary English classrooms, foreign language classes, and some elements have been translated by enthusiastic teachers into French, German, Spanish and even Gaelic.

The approach is planned around a weekly timetable and provides a flexible structure that gives teachers freedom and ownership, whilst still offering consistency across the school. Tools are provided to ensure that comprehension tasks and questions are not only challenging, but specific and relevant to the texts being studied and the needs of the class. There is an emphasis on 'joining the dots' of the learning, and making appropriate links to the rest of the curriculum and reading and writing.

When *Reflective Reading* is introduced to children, there should be an almost immediate improvement in motivation towards reading. Despite being challenging, the tasks and activities are engaging and game-like; enjoyment and choice is built in. Progression is obvious; children learn how to discuss, write, and develop comprehension answers (and questions) with increasing sophistication and independence. Variety of text type and subject also ensures that interest is maintained, with everything from stories, to non-fiction, to films, adverts and picture books being used as reading material.

## CLOSING THE GAP

Reflective Reading is based on the Scottish curriculum, Curriculum for Excellence, good practice, and current research. If you are looking for an intervention to improve school results, or to 'close gaps' that may exist between cohorts of children, it is useful to know that reading comprehension strategies have been identified by the Education Endowment Foundation as a cost effective, proven method for improving attainment. In addition, Reflective Reading uses small group work, focused teaching and mixed ability groupings (where appropriate) which also help to 'close the gap'.

N.B. Reflective Reading focuses on the comprehension aspect of reading. Every school should also have in place a high quality phonics programme to ensure all children can decode effortlessly and accurately; good decoding is a prerequisite for good comprehension.

## YOUR READING JOURNEY

Do you remember the moment you started reading? For some, it was a eureka moment; a defining memory of an independent discovery of the secrets of the printed page. Others cannot recall a time in their lives when they couldn't read—even in their earliest days. For most though, myself included, there was no magic moment—I simply don't remember the time, the place, the book. I suspect that is because for me, and many others, it was something that I didn't struggle with. Everyone has a different reading story, a different journey, and in the same way, each child in your class will have their own unique path to understanding print. But as we will see in Chapter 2: *How to Build a Reader*, this journey shouldn't be left to chance encounters.

What I do remember clearly though, are certain books; books that were like beacons of my childhood. The first was *A Brother for Momoko* by Chihiro Iwasaki that my mum read to me before my brother was born. This book had such an impact that, despite being only four at the time, I can remember the title, some of the pictures and even some of the words, almost 40 years later. When the newborn baby arrives home he was described as 'tiny, soft and warm'. Only a fragment of text, but I can even recall my mum's intonation of those few words. Sadly, I don't know what happened to the original book, but I did manage to track down a copy a few years ago. It is now a family heirloom.

At school, I was lucky and was introduced to everything from *Charlotte's Web* to poetry in Scots to Shakespeare. But it was A *Gift from Winklesea* by Helen Cresswell, read to us by Mrs Clarke in Primary 5, that stayed with me most. It is one I have read to almost every class I have taught; I hope some of them remember it as fondly as I do.

Anne sharing 'A Brother for Momoko' with her children, Harris and Lauren.

> "I cannot remember the books I've read any more than all the meals I have eaten; even so, they have made me."

**RALPH WALDO EMERSON**

The quote above is one of my favourites. I love the idea that what we read, makes us who we are, that '*you are what you read*'.

What books are you made out of? How did your journey with books begin? Were you reading your own *Ladybird* library in your bedroom or did you want to be the sixth member of *The Famous Five*? Did an American series seduce you, such as *Sweet Valley High*, *Babysitters Club* or *Point Horror?* Or are you young enough to have started with *Harry Potter?* Maybe you were reading Judy Blume behind the bike sheds… Or was that just me?

Which book has had a lasting impact; has left its imprint? Perhaps it was read to you as a child, or at school, or maybe it was one of the first books you read independently?

My book beacon is...

OK. I know you're not really going to fill in any blanks in this book, but let's pretend. Imagine the name of your book sitting there on the post-it note...

My book beacon is 'The Gingerbread Man'! Yum!

Have you shared this book memory with your class? (Or with your own children if you're a parent?) Are you creating reading moments with your class—ones that will become their beacons and shine despite the passing of time?

Different books will speak to different children; we need to make sure that we're reading and sharing a variety of high quality, engaging texts in the classroom—something we'll explore in depth throughout this book.

## THE DEFINITION OF 'TEXT'

In Scotland, *Curriculum for Excellence* introduced a new, more robust and future-proofed 'definition of text'. It is no longer adequate to say that reading = books. Reading now refers to anything that children 'read, listen or watch'. This means that the notion of 'text' is a wide one—and it includes everything from books, adverts, leaflets, graphs, maps and charts to films, trailers, YouTube, audio books, social media, recipes, emails and more. Children should be reading these sorts of text—and where appropriate, they should be writing and creating these sorts of texts too.

While this change is a welcome one, as it ensures that teachers use texts which are relevant and reflect reading in today's society, it is also important that books and more 'traditional' texts do not become displaced. While digital texts can be explored in the classroom and games, films and adverts can provide engagement, equity of access, and valuable discussion, ultimately children need to be able read and comprehend pages of print confidently. The only way to do this is through practice and engagement with texts composed of continuous prose, which can provide challenge through increasing sophistication and length, to help build reading fluency and stamina.

So while it is true that 'anything goes' when it comes to format, care should be taken to ensure that texts used have inherent value and not just surface appeal. For example, tapping into children's interests can be a useful tactic and reading about the latest

## THE DEFINITION OF 'TEXT' IN CURRICULUM FOR EXCELLENCE

'A text is the medium through which ideas, experiences, opinions and information can be communicated.'

**Example of texts:**

novels, short stories, plays, poems
reference texts
the spoken word
charts, maps, graphs and timetables
advertisements, promotional leaflets
comics, newspapers and magazines
CVs, letters and emails
films, games and TV programmes
labels, signs and posters
recipes, manuals and instructions
reports and reviews
text messages, blogs and social networking sites
web pages, catalogues and directories

CURRICULUM FOR EXCELLENCE
LITERACY AND ENGLISH
PRINCIPLES AND PRACTICE

must-have game or playground craze is sure-fire strategy to get them on-board, but we must go beyond these gateway texts and push their curiosity and capacity for reading and learning further.

Some texts that are shared in the classroom will purely be for pleasure, but when choosing texts for study some good questions to ask are: Why *this* text? What can it teach us that is of value? Does it add to our understanding of language, grammar, the writer's craft, text type or genre features? Does it add to our subject knowledge in another curricular area?

In an ideal world, every text should be high quality, high interest with high payback. Consider: does *this* text deserve a slot in my heaving timetable? Or, to subvert L'Oreal's catchphrase: *is it worth it?*

## READING REFLECTIONS: A SELF-EVALUATION

Obviously, the very fact that you are even reading this book right now shows that you are a reflective practitioner. Perhaps you have a desire to improve or to enhance how you teach reading at the moment, or perhaps you seek to be reassured that what you're already doing isn't any different to what is in this book, or maybe you're searching for a whole-school solution to improve attainment and motivation for reading too?

Before diving into *Reflective Reading* in depth, it is important to review what your own classroom practice looks like, to recognise what you're already doing, and to consider the areas that may be ripe for improvement. The Self-Evaluation on the next few pages takes around five minutes to fill in and it will encourage you to think about reading from different perspectives. First it looks at issues which concern the whole school and its 'reading ethos', next it considers how reading is approached in your own classroom, where you are the manager. Finally, on a more personal level, it examines your own relationship with reading.

Simply read each section, and for each statement, give yourself a 'tick' if you can say 'Yes—I'm doing that!', a 'dot' if you're doing it, but only some of the time, and a cross (don't worry—no-one's looking!) if it's something that you hadn't considered before or you're not doing currently. There are four boxes next to each statement—one for each term, so you can track progress over the school year or session.

## WHOLE-SCHOOL ISSUES

| | T1 | T2 | T3 | T4 |
|---|---|---|---|---|
| We take part in national and local reading events and initiatives such as World Book Day and the Summer Reading Challenge. | | | | |
| We value reading. Our reading ethos is apparent in our daily life and work and can be felt all year round. | | | | |
| Community members regularly read to classes or share a text and their reading habits with us. | | | | |
| Our school library is a beloved and well-used space. It is well-stocked, and welcoming; it always has new books on offer. | | | | |
| We subscribe to regular newspapers and magazines. | | | | |
| Where possible, we visit our local library and know our local librarian well. | | | | |
| We organise our own events to promote reading such as Book Swaps and Bedtime Story Evenings. | | | | |
| We engage with authors and illustrators through school visits and/or live internet talks. (Such as Authors Live from the Scottish Book Trust) | | | | |
| We have an active Book Club, run by children. | | | | |
| We have a staff Research Group to read and discuss educational research. | | | | |
| Reading books and resources are fit for purpose, engaging, and available in sufficient quantities. | | | | |
| Phonically decodable books are used for beginning reading instruction and for intervention purposes. | | | | |
| We identify children that may at risk of reading failure and ensure that robust, research-informed interventions are in place to teach them to read, write and spell as a matter of urgency. | | | | |

| TEACHING, LEARNING AND CLASSROOM ROUTINE | T1 | T2 | T3 | T4 |
|---|---|---|---|---|
| I enable children to choose texts for reading for pleasure. I allow choice in texts for study when appropriate. | | | | |
| I ensure that children have access to a wide range of high quality, high interest texts within the classroom setting. | | | | |
| Our classroom has an established reading culture: part of every day is used for silent personal reading. (ERIC / DEAR) | | | | |
| We start every morning with a poem, joke, quote or song. | | | | |
| I read and share a chapter a day from our class novel for pleasure. | | | | |
| I provide a balanced diet of reading material and a variety of text types / genres as outlined in the 'definition of text' as well as Scottish texts and texts in Scots. (if appropriate) | | | | |
| I choose texts that links to our learning across the curriculum e.g. social studies, RME, science etc. | | | | |
| We have a wall display that records the different sorts of texts we encounter through our reading. | | | | |
| I have an awareness of children's literature and authors including classic and contemporary favourites. | | | | |
| I use a variety of strategies and methods for reading including e.g. Literacy Circles, Book Detectives, DARTs, Critical Skills, Reciprocal Reading, and Reflective Reading. | | | | |
| I encourage deep thinking, critical study, exploring themes that go beyond the text. | | | | |
| I make explicit links to how our reading links to our learning, our other reading, and the relevance of the text to our own lives and the wider world. | | | | |
| Where possible, extended writing tasks are linked to our reading in class e.g. to a Short Read text that we have studied as a whole class. | | | | |
| I provide research-informed instruction for children in my class who are struggling with their basic literacy skills, using the evidence-based phonics or intervention programme my school has adopted. | | | | |

A downloadable pdf version of this document is included in the digital resources if you wish to print it out and complete this evaluation as a whole staff as a basis for discussion.

## TEACHER AS READER

| | T1 | T2 | T3 | T4 |
|---|---|---|---|---|
| I model reading behaviours and join the children when they take part in personal, silent reading. | | | | |
| I share my reading habits and invite others to share theirs, including other adults / visitors to the classroom. | | | | |
| I model reflective reading and thinking and express my opinions and thoughts about my reading. | | | | |
| I encourage enthusiasm for reading; demonstrating how texts in all forms, for every purpose, can inform us, entertain us, and enrich our lives. | | | | |
| I enjoy reading in all forms covering a wide range of texts and text types; I am a reader. | | | | |
| I read and access professional texts, including educational research, to help develop and inform my practice. | | | | |
| I find time for myself to read what I enjoy, whatever that may be. (Silent reading can reduce stress!) | | | | |

Now, I know you're eager to skip on to the next part, but before you do—please—read over your evaluation. If you had to select three action points from section 1 'Whole School Issues' that you would see as a priority, what would they be?

Have another look at sections two and three, if you had to choose three action points for yourself and your classroom or teaching, what would they be?

Now you have a handy Six Point Action Plan! Hopefully, in the following pages you will find advice, ideas and activities to help you begin to address them. Before moving on though, we'll address some issues raised in the self-evaluation.

Hey! Who wants to hear my Six Point Action Plan? Anyone? Guys?

## My Six Point Action Plan

1.
2.
3.

## CATCHING CABBAGES

So how was it for you? Did you have a lot of dots and crosses? Unless reading has been a development priority in your school, you are likely to have a list of action points. Once, during a *Reflective Reading* conference with teachers, I asked the group how they'd found the self-assessment. Two lovely teachers at the front said 'We're ashamed!'. I tried to reassure them by explaining that the list was aspirational and designed to generate discussion. 'It's worse than that, Anne,' they replied. Worse? Why? 'Because we used to do this stuff'. And a murmur of recognition passed round the room. So, what's happened? Why aren't we doing the good stuff anymore? And the collective response is always the same: time.

To say that the school curriculum is busy would be a gross understatement. The plate of primary teachers has never been so full, or heavy. We have around 22 hours a week of actual teaching time, but if you consider everything we feel we should be doing, you will struggle to fit that into a two week timetable—let alone one. Starting with curricular areas: Expressive arts, Health and wellbeing, Languages, Mathematics, Religious and moral education, Sciences, Social studies and Technologies, which on the surface doesn't sound too bad—if that was all we had to do. The problem is the *other stuff*, the *extra bits* that are thrown on top of everything else—or as I like to call them—*cabbages*.

If you were around in the 70s you might remember a children's TV programme called *Crackerjack*… At the end of the show, the contestants would have a chance to win prizes and whatever you managed to hold on to, you got to keep. But there was an added difficulty, people weren't just giving you prizes—they were piling cabbages on too. Drop a prize, or a cabbage—you're out! Your

hands are full and people are still giving you cabbages; that's what it feels like at times in a primary school.

Everything from daily toothbrushing in class, to enterprise and finance education, charity work as responsible citizens, sustainability, eco-schools, gardens and outdoor learning to parental involvement, school trips, important visitors, Golden Time—and this term don't forget the book swap, jumble sale, assembly, wall display or end-of-term show… and that's just the tip of the *iceberg*.

New cabbage varieties are always being introduced. Recent additions in Scotland include: 1+2 languages (that is your mother tongue plus two foreign ones), walk a mile a day (this doesn't count toward your weekly quota of two hours of quality P.E.) and in England a cabbage for computer coding from the age of 5 also made an appearance. Not that this stuff isn't important—it is—but our time is finite and we need to cut our cloth accordingly.

*death by cabbage*

I believe that in the quest to 'do it all' we can end up 'window dressing'—and the time for quality teaching and learning with daily, consecutive practice in our core skills, such as maths and English, is being eroded.

We need to re-align the balance, re-introduce rigour to our classrooms with protected time for core teaching and learning of basic skills. We need to prioritise our way through the clutter of the curriculum and realise that teaching cannot be carried out entirely through games, group work and discovery learning. Schools need to take control of their curriculums before the cabbages do. On that note, let's look at two cabbages that I do consider to be *essential*…

## WE NEED TO TALK ABOUT ERIC

Does your classroom have an established reading culture? Is part of every day used for silent personal reading? It doesn't matter what you call it, as long as you're doing it!

**ERIC** (Everyone Reading in Class),
**DEAR** (Drop Everything and Read)
**SSR** (Self-Selected Reading)
**DIRT** (Daily Independent Reading Time)

and my new favourite, that I stole off the internet...

**BEAR**\* (Be Excited About Reading) \*teddy bears are optional

Depending on which age/stage you're working in, 10-15 minutes of personal reading time every day in class is achievable and the effects can be transformative. At the beginning of the day it provides a secure, quiet and calming routine before launching into the work that lies ahead. Texts should, of course, be chosen by the children. When you can, read silently alongside the class. When you can't, even having your own 'reading for pleasure' material on the desk sends a positive message. (If it's *Fifty Shades of Grey*, best keep that in your bag. :D)

If ERIC's the best way to start the day, then the best way to finish the day is by reading to the class and sharing a chapter of a novel together (or a picture book if you're further down the school).

Never, ever, feel guilty about taking time to read to your class. You can justify it every day of the week. You may be the \*only\* person that reads to that child in their whole life. You are improving their vocabulary, modelling fluency and expression, widening their literary horizons (do pick books that they are unlikely to choose or read for themselves) and most

importantly, showing them that reading is rewarding, fun, and worth it.

Make no mistake, in class, I am a bit of a task master—but punctuate the day with reading at either end—and you have a little parcel of loveliness. Everyone goes home feeling good and is thirsty for more the next day.

### WHAT ABOUT ACCELERATED READER?

Sometimes teachers can be a bit sniffy about the AR programme. Personally, I'm all for anything that promotes reading for enjoyment and can help motivate children. I've seen it used to great effect in many primary schools. It certainly provides a solution for busy teachers and helps to manage ERIC book choices effectively. Also, because AR provides an organisational system and book suggestions—schools using AR tend to have well-managed, nicely stocked libraries with a wide range of books on offer.

Here comes the 'but'...

I feel AR should be used for ERIC time books only—as an add-on. It should not be used instead of reading books, novels or whatever is actually being used for the teaching and learning of reading in class.

To enable high quality discussion, teaching and learning, children need to be sharing and reading a text at the same time e.g. as a reading group or as a class (where appropriate/possible).

JONNY WALKER

# Nostalgia as Pebbledash

**In this witty and wonderfully written article, Jonny Walker explores the nature of our school memories, from the often strange and inexplicable things that stick, to the extraordinary power that reading can have in the classroom. He describes the peculiar quality of moments that are, at the same time, for every day and forever; he captures and encapsulates *the feeling of reading*.**

Nostalgia guides us, and not always in the most helpful directions.

My memories of primary school are scattergun, a smattering of half-forgotten moments. I remember vividly the experience of queueing up at my Year 3 teacher's knees, waiting to ask her my burning question, my chest puffed up with the early symptoms of the kind of misplaced academical snootiness that would characterise much of my education since:

"Can you help with a spelling please? It's a very long word."

"What is the word, Jonathan?"

"Heck–tick."

I remember looking around to see who overheard this burst of brilliance. Most of my memories play out like this. They are mere glimpses of oddness: they are more photograph than video clip.

In Reception I told someone they had ants in their pants and they cried. I thought I had fallen in love once during a P.E. lesson whilst playing piggy in the middle on the school field. My friend started a small fire to the cloak room. Somebody said a racist word in fitness club. In Year 4 the new girl put her hands down the back of her pants and encouraged people to smell it. The Deputy Head stopped me crying in the lunch hall by winking at me and teaching me how to wink. I proudly boasted of *'being the boy who likes every pudding'.* I had a *Spice Girls* keyring and a sticker of Sally Gunnell. A potter's wheel pinned me to the floor of the car park. The teacher mispronounced organism and some other children started laughing; I didn't get the joke until like two years later. In Year 2, I played with a Year 1 girl who was often mean to me, and I didn't know her name so I called her *Little Blue Riding Hood*. The substitute teacher was rumoured to be another species and the music teacher drove a yellow Fiat Panda. When the ball went out of bounds for a throw-in, I would always be honest if I touched it last, and my team would shout at me for being an idiot as a result.

The fact that these memories remain as shards and as fragments does not undermine their impact. As far as I am concerned, these kinds of things shaped me as much as anything else I clearly learned but do not remember learning, such as how to do my shoelaces, where to put a question mark, how to measure an angle or the sequence of the Tudor monarchs.

## MEMORIES OF THE CARPET

One set of my memories is unaffected by this fragmentation and blurring. Memories of reading are the most concrete ones I have from school. These stayed with me and struck me as important, even at the time. They attest to the peculiar power of reading.

I say peculiar intentionally; the power of reading is a strange one. In my classrooms as a child—and now as a teacher—the opening or closing of a book can be enough to immediately alter the mood of a room, to calm or madden the class as if they were one body and to give the impression of stopping time.

As a kid, when we visited the library, we were allowed to browse for ages, and the teacher generally left us be. I don't actually remember them being there, but I know they were. We had about a five minute walk to cover to get to the library, but at the time it felt so much longer. An old man called Cyril would sometimes stop us all on our walk through the estate and give out mint imperials. We would arrive, crunching the mints, and would lug our completed books up onto the library desk, before running around. Lots of the kids did anyway.

I had my slow route planned which I tended to stick to. I had a look at the tapes and CDs first, then moved to comics, then to the section of adult non-fiction

books I was allowed to have a look at, before moving around the kids section to the non-fiction. I would often end the session standing in the Young Adult section, feeling as cocky as I did when I was declaring my knowledge of the word 'hectic'.

Certain books stand out to me, and seeing the covers now still transports me back. One of these is *Blabbermouth* by Morris Gleitzman. Another is a retelling of *Ivanhoe*, which I couldn't really understand. Another, which I didn't ever read but would always look for was *Johnny and the Bomb* by Terry Pratchett.

Back in school, the most salient memories of reading seemed to be tied to the five minutes before lunchtime. Perhaps the knowledge that food was on its way was what heightened my engagement for this time period, but I feel as though if all of my primary school memories were to wither, the last one to fade into the ether would be the experience of looking up into the yellowed mouth of our partially-deaf regular cover teacher as she bellowed *Please Mrs Butler* at a shuddering volume.

At the time, this teacher appeared to us to be absolutely ancient, but with retrospect, she was probably only pushing 45. She had her reading glasses on a chain, and when she put them on, her eyes were like the headlights on a Volkswagen Beetle.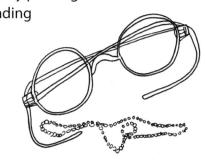

In my mind's eye, I imagine her to be about 14 feet tall, but this is because all of my memories of her now come from the position of me on a small chair gawping up at her.

When she would say the words 'THIS BOY DEREK DREW', she would get so much louder and quite often a ball of bubbling spit would land on the table next to me. Her breath was old coffee. Once it landed on my hand.

We wouldn't vary the poems. It would always be the same poem and the predictability of it made it no less exciting. It was exciting in the way that the predictability of Christmas or that moment you get out of the door at playtime is exciting. Novelty was not required.

## THE BRINGER OF HUSH

Reading was, for me, mostly a personal experience until I was a bit older. In Year 7, I made a friend for the first time who read lots of books and had a house full of them. She would lend me hers and we would read things that were not commonly read by kids of our age. I would go around on a Saturday so we could read the Guardian Weekend supplement.

I gradually came to understand the power of sharing these stories, and how recommendations and book chat could be really exciting. My friend showed me books she had read that I had never heard of, and I devoured them. Books like *The Ringmaster's Daughter* and *The Solitaire Mystery* changed my life, in a quite tangible way.

As we fast-forward now into my own classroom, I am trying to recreate that gentle sense of mundane awe that I felt when I first saw my friend's bookshelf in her bedroom when I was about 12. I could

point to any one of them and she could talk to me about it. They were tattered and torn, well-thumbed and drawn on. They had notes and comments, even sketches, alongside the text. The books were very much in the world of the living, unlike the copy of *Johnny and the Bomb* that absorbed dust on the bottom shelf of the library.

That lilting memory of the descending calm, as the supply teacher would loudly clear her throat ahead of our daily *Ahlberging*, glows in my mind every time I rotate my swivel chair with a dramatic flourish; the kids know this means I am going into my chest of drawers where my copy of AF Harrold's *The Imaginary* is.

They are pining for the story so badly, I fear we may have to deal with withdrawal symptoms once it is over. I have been working with what is going to be my class now, for just five whole days. Already, our reading time is sacred. This class is much like one I had a few years ago, who I loved for their character, humour and temperament, at the same time as deeply resenting how difficult this made my life.

"These are all great questions Year 5, but for this next bit, please no more hands up and no more questions. OK, so in thi... your hand is up... I said, no questions."

"I don't have a question, I want to make a statement."

They are effervescent.
Thus far, at this early stage as I am working out the class, the kids, the personalities and the dynamics, my one reliable technique, my one faultless and effortless routine, has been to slowly raise *The Imaginary* aloft.

As if it is some kind of conch, they gather around me, settle and anticipate. Some of them confided that they found the bedroom 'hide and seek' scene really scary, and Emily Gravett's illustrations certainly helped this along, but every single child— even those who were looking at me from between their fingers, huddled at the thought of what might happen next—every last one of them was quiet, looking and waiting.

This is the feeling of reading. This is that transcendent quality that moves beyond talk of grammar, punctuation, vocabulary, spelling and sentence structures. This feeling hints at the truth that stories are more than just the sum of their parts. Even within an engaging curriculum, I have yet to find anything that can create the same kind of fervent buzz, the same kind of verve, as does a story well told.

Whilst the 'best teacher' is a universal platitude given to any adult in a lanyard, I liked the idea that this sketch—which I found in the bin at end of the day—is how the kid experienced it: a bearded egg with a gesticulating club hand, reading a scary book in a place outside the space-time continuum. I'm probably reading too much into it...

Jonny Walker is a Primary Assistant Headteacher at Park Primary School in East London. He is a self-confessed children's book hoarder.

Tweet him:

@jonnywalker_edu
@MyBookIsNice

Read and follow his brilliant blogs:

mybookisnice.wordpress.com
jonnywalkerteaching.wordpress.com

JONNY WALKER

# 15 *FUN IDEAS* TO GET EVERYONE READING

**1.** Take part in a reading event that's new for your school; celebrate a national event or make up your own.

How about a 'Poetry Picnic', 'Shakespeare on the Lawn', or a 'Reading Rammy'* to celebrate Scottish books, authors and texts in Scots?**

**2.** Have a whole-school competition to come up with a new acronym and/or door poster for ERIC time.

**3.** Share reviews & promote new books at assembly before they are added to the library.

**4.** Curate and share your own school 100 Must-Read Books List.

**5.** Have a Bedtime Story Evening with pyjamas, hot chocolate, hot dogs, torches, sleeping bags and plenty of stories.

**6.** Make a 'Place to Read at Playtime' in the playground; it can be a reading den, a book nook, or even a picnic bench.

**7.** Set up a special Storyteller chair... Have an enchanted Story evening opening ceremony.

**8.** Have a story a day every day at lunchtime in the library or outside—led by older children or a community member.

**9.** Start a Book Club, Comic Club or a Film Club: for children, teachers or families.

**10.** Don't forget non-fiction; celebrate and share 'This book taught me...'

**11.** Design & set some school reading challenges; reward winners and record breakers with reading related prizes.

**12.** Fundraise with a sponsored read for a reading charity, for a new library, or for new books.

**13.** Have an author event or watch one on YouTube.

**14.** Arrange permanent Book Swap Zones for children, teachers, and parents.

**15.** Have a 'My Favourite Book', 'Currently Reading...' or 'Extreme Reading' display; invite different children, teachers, school staff and community members to contribute.

## LET'S HAVE A READING RAMMY!

*rammy (noun; Scottish) a quarrel or brawl e.g.'they started a rammy at the pub/disco/TeachMeet'

**other nationalities and languages are available. Ideal for promoting any languages that are important in your context/community

## THE IMPORTANCE OF READING FOR PLEASURE

Time for some good news: it is impossible to dispute the importance of reading for pleasure. As adults, teachers, and parents, we must do whatever we can to encourage reading as a choice, as a hobby, as a habit. Reading for pleasure's many benefits are well documented by research; children who regularly read for fun will not only improve their vocabulary and spelling—it can even be linked to an improvement in maths performance.

Crucially, reading for pleasure has been shown to be more important for cognitive development in children from the ages of 10-16—than their parents' level of education and PISA (*Programme for International Student Assessment, 2009*) survey shows that increasing reading engagement could mitigate 30% of the attainment gap associated with socio-economic disadvantage. With the UK being one of the most unequal societies in the world and a stubborn and shameful poverty related attainment gap, the fact that reading for pleasure can actually mitigate the home circumstances of some of our children, is something we cannot afford to ignore.

The educational benefits associated with reading for pleasure are enormous: better vocabulary, spelling, comprehension, grammar, and writing ability. But so are other perhaps less tangible advantages, such as positive attitudes towards reading and improved self-confidence as a reader. Reading for fun can also foster empathy as we experience and come to understand different cultures, lives, and points of view.

Want to know more? There's lots of fascinating, easy to read research about reading for pleasure including children's choices and motivations. Start with the references section in the appendix.

### CAN READING REDUCE STRESS?

A small-scale study carried out by Dr David Lewis in 2009 suggested that six minutes of reading can reduce stress levels by more than two thirds. Reading was deemed better and quicker for calming the nerves than listening to music, going for a walk or having a cup of tea!

N.B. More research is required to have conclusive proof, but who could argue with Dr Lewis's statement that 'losing yourself in a book is the ultimate relaxation.' Hear, hear!

An aspect of reading for pleasure that I feel is often neglected is the fact that reading makes you smarter. It's so obvious, but reading improves your general knowledge. And that knowledge of the world is crucial to our comprehension and understanding of texts we encounter. Feeling dizzy? It's a virtuous cycle: reading increases intellect which increases comprehension of what you read.

Lots of evidence suggests that independent reading is the best predictor of reading achievement, in other words, there is a positive relationship between how often children read, how much they enjoy reading, and their attainment levels. Unsurprisingly, children who enjoy reading do more of it. This is why I believe it's critical to ensure that every child can read confidently, fluently — with automaticity. If reading is a 'chore' and something they don't enjoy, or don't feel they are good at, they will never seek it out as a pastime of their own free will. Hence the importance of getting reading right at the start of school—and that brings us neatly onto Chapter 2 and *How to Build A Reader*.

# CHAPTER 2

# How to Build a Reader

# How to Build a Reader

I cdnuolt blveiee that I cluod aulaclty uesdnatnrd what I was rdanieg. The phaonmneal pweor of the hmuan mnid, aoccdrnig to rscheearch at Cmabrigde Uinervtisy, maens it dseno't mtaetr in what oerdr the ltteres in a word are in, the olny iproamtnt tihng is that the frsit and last ltteer are in the rghit pclae. The rset can be a taotl mses and you can still raed it whotuit a pboerlm.

This is bcuseae the huamn mnid deos not raed ervey lteter by istlef, but the word as a wlohe.

**Ture or Fasle?**

## IF YOU CAN READ THIS YOU HAVE A STRANGE MIND...

**R**emember this? It used to do the rounds by email, but every once in a while it pops up on Twitter and Facebook. Can you read it? Go on, have a go, I won't watch. Now I want you to decide… is it true? Or is it false?

'I couldn't believe that I could actually understand what I was reading. The phenomenal power of the human mind, according to research at Cambridge University, means that it doesn't matter what order the letters in a word are in, the only important thing is that the first and last letter are in the right place.
The rest can be a total mess and you can still read it without a problem.
This is because the human mind does not read every letter by itself, but the word as a whole.'

Hmmm. What did you say? Hands up for true. Oh, quite a few of you. *OK,* hands up for false… Is your hand up? Well, being brave has paid off. You're the only person reading this book right now that said 'false'—and it's the RIGHT answer! Well done!

This meme is in fact a hoax. It has nothing at all to do with Cambridge University—and while what it suggests might actually *feel* true, it is in fact, entirely wrong. Eye gaze studies have shown that we *do* actually read every letter by itself; your brain just does it incredibly quickly and, as it's a subconscious process, you're entirely unaware of it. It 'feels easy' for you to read the meme—but you are an accomplished reader and you're able to solve this puzzle very quickly. It would be quite different for a struggling reader.

So much is going on when we read. We're recognising letters and words, automatically, rapidly. We're making connections to our prior knowledge, using that and the context to aid our understanding of the whole text. We also have to self-monitor our reading to see if we're 'getting it'—or if we need to go back a few sentences to check our understanding. If we're reading aloud, we have to attend to punctuation, expression and speed, while taking our audience into account. If that wasn't enough, at the same time, we are reflecting on, questioning, evaluating the text in our minds. Even as you're reading this book you will have a running commentary going on in your head. It might be saying things like 'I don't get it. What's the point of this meme?', 'Oh yes, I remember this!', or 'Hurry up and tell us how to build a reader!'. That little voice in your head is you, speaking to yourself. This is the voice we use for thinking (and reading and writing)—I like to call it the 'Mini-Me.'

Here comes your first piece of homework. Yes, there is homework. Introduce your class to the concept of their 'Mini-Me'—the thinking voice that they have inside their head. Get everyone to make their own 'Mini-Me'—it's simply a laminated character or hand-drawn figure glued or taped to the top of a lollipop stick. Let them choose who is going to represent them: it can be a cartoon character, a real-life role model or even a little mini photo of themselves. Teachers should also create their own 'Mini-Me' for demonstration purposes. (Mine is a photo of a very lovely Nigella Lawson on a lollipop stick!)

'Mini-Me's are good for two things. Firstly, they protect self-esteem. In the classroom, children will often only contribute an answer to a question if they're 99% sure they know they have the one you're looking for. But if children have a Mini-Me, that can take the pressure off as they can either take credit for the right answer, or distance themselves from the wrong answer. It's not them that's 'wrong'—it's Minecraft Steve—or Nigella.

'Mini-Me's at West Linton PS

The second thing that 'Mini-Me's are good for is making the implicit, explicit. If you think about reading, most of it is taking place silently in our heads. As we read, our 'inner reader' translates the visual cues of the writing on the page into sounds and words. The 'inner reader' is also our gatekeeper: reading aloud, thinking our thoughts and questioning what we read. It decides if we should trust our sources, believe our narrator or decide if something is fact or fiction.

We must ensure that every inner reader is alert, activated and capable of the reading challenges ahead. Find opportunities to ask 'What does your Mini-Me think?' 'How do they know?' Use the Mini-Me to reveal reasoning and encourage learning dialogue that will show how we draw conclusions and find the answers to reading questions. We've become very good in maths at asking 'How did you get that answer?', 'Did anyone do it a different way?' to explore and model possible solutions. We need to develop the same habit of discussing answers to reading questions, while referring back to the text. Teachers that have been using 'Mini-Me's report that children are enthusiastic about them and even request their use in other subjects— particularly in maths.

## TEACHING READING IS ROCKET SCIENCE

Every child needs to be taught how to read, not only to access the curriculum and improve knowledge, but to benefit from the wider opportunities that reading for pleasure offers. Reading is not like talking—it doesn't just happen naturally. You will learn to talk—as long as people are speaking to you. Reading is different—reading is an invention (and a fairly recent one in evolutionary terms) —and as such, we have to help children understand how this invention works.

Children will not simply start reading and writing when they reach some magical developmental milestone—they need to be taught. To quote Dr Louisa Moats, 'Reading is the fundamental skill upon which all formal education depends,' for this reason, teaching all children to read (write and spell) should be a priority in every primary school.

> "Reading is the fundamental skill upon which all formal education depends. Research now shows that a child who doesn't learn the reading basics early is unlikely to learn them at all."
>
> DR LOUISA C. MOATS
>
> TEACHING READING IS ROCKET SCIENCE
> What Expert Teachers of Reading Should Know and Be Able To Do

We should be aiming to teach 100% of our children to read—and we should expect to get very close. (It will only be in 2%-3% where children will have profound difficulties that this will not be possible.) Currently, in most English speaking countries, it is 'normal' to see 15%-20% of the children in each class not doing as well as their peers when it comes to reading. It is not that what we are doing at the moment isn't working, but crucially, it's not working for **every** child. We need a new normal. Leading-edge practice and research-informed reading instruction is what can make the difference; we must do all we can to support our teachers and our children to achieve these vital literacy skills.

Reading is a complex skill. To analyse it further, it helps to break it down into its two component parts:

**decoding + comprehension = reading**

Decoding refers to being able to read words and to 'lift them off the page'. Comprehension (understanding what the words mean) in this case refers to oral comprehension e.g. if the text was read to the child would they understand it? Both aspects of reading are essential and neither is sufficient on its own. This formula is known as **The Simple View of Reading** (Gough and Tunmer, 1986).

In diagram format (see opposite page) it is extremely useful for diagnosing which aspect of reading children may be struggling with; this in turn enables teachers to provide instruction and practice that will help ensure progress in the required area.

Let's try placing a child in your class, or a child you know well, on the SVoR (Simple View of Reading) chart. First, ask the question: is this child good at decoding or poor at decoding? Can they lift the words off the page easily, fluently and accurately? Or are they struggling, with reading that is slow, stilted and laboured. Now you know if they are going to be on the left (POOR) or right (GOOD) side of the chart.

Next, consider their comprehension. How do you know if they are good or poor? Do you need to give them a test? No. As this refers to oral comprehension you simply have to imagine you reading a text to the child. For argument's sake, let's imagine that you're reading *Charlie and the Chocolate Factory* aloud. Would this child understand what you're reading? If they do, then there isn't a problem with comprehension.

Now you know which quadrant they fall into on the chart… and know you know where the issue (or issues) lie. Most frequently, children that are struggling with reading are actually

struggling with decoding—with getting the words off the page.

## GOOD DECODING-GOOD COMPREHENSION

I can read text fluently, accurately and at speed. (I may, or may not be able to use expression effectively.) I can understand what I read and am able to answer simple literal questions about main points or events in a text. I can also answer questions that require 'reading between the lines' or inference. I am able to give my thoughts and opinions about a text.

I am a reader—I am good at both decoding and comprehension. I can decode automatically and understand whatever I am reading. Good job!

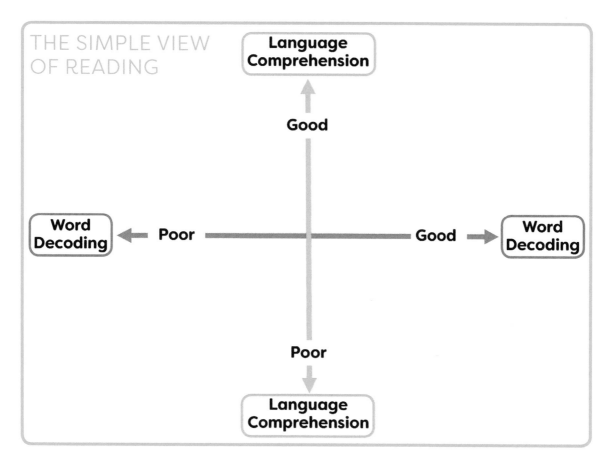

THE SIMPLE VIEW OF READING

Language Comprehension

Good

Word Decoding ← Poor — Good → Word Decoding

Poor

Language Comprehension

The Simple View of Reading, Gough & Tunmer, 1986. The Rose Review, 2006
R=DxC reading= decoding x comprehension

### GOOD DECODING-POOR COMPREHENSION

The issue here is with comprehension. It is important to provide a literacy rich environment, supported by lots of talking, listening and discussion. Focus on enriching vocabulary by examining new words and their meanings. Provide lots of reading time and material; include non-fiction texts to enhance knowledge about the world. Questioning should ensure that the main points/events of a text have been understood. Support and model how to cope with inferential and evaluative questions.

### POOR DECODING-GOOD COMPREHENSION

(This is the most common quadrant for strugglers.)
My reading is slow and laboured. I am struggling to lift the words off the page. I often guess at words and make mistakes. Although I am slow at reading, I understand and can explain, describe and answer questions about what is happening in the text.
The problem here is with decoding. This must be addressed urgently. Assess how much of the alphabetic code is known; analyse knowledge of sounds/letters (grapheme/ phoneme correspondences) to identify where the gaps are. A systematic synthetic phonics programme will provide the necessary alphabetic code knowledge and practice in decoding/blending for reading and encoding/ segmenting for spelling.

### POOR DECODING-POOR COMPREHENSION

The issue here is with both decoding and comprehension. Decoding must be addressed urgently. Assess how much of the alphabetic code is known; analyse

knowledge of sounds/letters (grapheme/ phoneme correspondences) to identify where the gaps are. A systematic synthetic phonics programme will provide the necessary alphabetic code knowledge and practice in decoding/blending for reading and encoding/ segmenting for spelling. It is important to provide a literacy rich environment, supported by lots of talking, listening and discussion. Focus on enriching vocabulary by examining new words and their meanings. Provide lots of reading time and material; include non-fiction texts to enhance knowledge about the world. Questioning should ensure that the main points/events of a text have been understood. Support and model how to cope with inferential and evaluative questions.

The 'decision tree', or 'bi-furcating key', on the opposite page summarises this advice.

### THE SIMPLE VIEW OF READING: HOMEWORK

A valuable exercise is to plot all of the children in your class on the SVoR chart. You than have a handy, at-a-glance document that will show you who is struggling with what. This is a perfect document to hand on to the next teacher at the end of term as it gives them an instant snapshot of where everyone is at. If children have two (or more) languages you can plot them for each one using a different colour.

This homework is better still if you download or photocopy the SVoR chart and fill it in together as a staff and use it as a stimulus for discussion.

# Identifying Reading Problems

**phonics** forever

**START**

I can read text fluently, accurately and at speed. (I may, or may not be able to use expression effectively.)

 **No**

My reading is slow and laboured. I am struggling to lift the words off the page. I often guess at words and make mistakes.

**Yes**

Although I am slow at reading, I understand and can explain, describe and answer questions about what is happening in the text.

**Yes**

The problem here is with decoding. **This must be addressed urgently.**

It is essential to analyse how much of the alphabetic code is known. Assess knowledge of sounds/ letters (grapheme / phoneme correspondences) to identify where the gaps are.

**A systematic synthetic phonics programme will provide the necessary alphabetic code knowledge and practice** in decoding/ blending for reading and encoding/ segmenting for spelling.

**No**

The issue here is with both decoding and comprehension

**Yes**

I can understand what I read and am able to answer simple literal questions about main points or events in a text. I can also answer questions that require 'reading between the lines' or inference. I am able to give my thoughts and opinions about a text.

 **No**

The issue here is with comprehension. **It is important to provide a literacy rich environment, supported by lots of talking, listening and discussion.** Focus on enriching vocabulary by examining new words and their meanings. Include non-fiction texts to enhance knowledge about the world. Questioning should ensure that the main points/ events of a text have been understood. Support & model how to cope with inferential and evaluative questions.

 **Yes**

I am a reader—I am good at both decoding and comprehension. I can decode automatically and understand whatever I am reading. Good job!

## using The Simple View of Reading

This flowchart is based on The Simple View of Reading. It will help you identify whether a child is struggling with word reading (decoding), comprehension—or with both. For further help and advice see www.dyslexics.org.uk

@anneglennie

## RECIPE FOR A READER

In order to 'build a reader' it is important to attend to both aspects of *The Simple View of Reading*, as outlined previously. We also want to ensure that we engage children's interest in reading—so that they become enthusiastic, confident, accomplished and motivated readers. Therefore, the recipe to 'build a reader' involves three essential ingredients:

- **Decoding / Word Recognition** (*Mechanics*): being able to read and 'lift the words off the page'
- **Comprehension** (*Meaning*): being able to understand what the words and text actually mean
- **Motivation**: being engaged and motivated—the desire to read and be a successful reader

It should also be noted that oral language skills underpin both aspects of reading (decoding/word recognition and comprehension) and its importance must not be underestimated. Teachers and parents need to read and talk lots with their children—providing high quality, rich literature experiences.

## The #yuMMMy Ingredients

## 1. MOTIVATION

Children need to be motivated readers—to see reading as something desirable, worthwhile and enjoyable—something that they want to be able to do. And it's never too early to start.

Songs, rhymes, stories and books are key from birth onwards—but there's even research that suggests reading to bumps is beneficial too as it is relaxing for mother and baby! Daily sharing of books throughout childhood encourages a love of language,

reading and a curiosity about words and the world around us. Listening to and discussing stories improves children's vocabularies, their empathy for others, and it also fires their imaginations.

Choice is also a factor in motivation to read. Where possible allow children to choose reading materials that interest them, so that they are reading for their own purposes. A good example of this is when my son, Harris, was about five years old. His preferred pocket money toy was a 'Trash Pack': a dirty plastic alien that came in its own little plastic bin. Disgusting? Yes. But how did it encourage reading? There were hundreds of creatures to collect, each had its own filthy name but to find out which member of the 'gross gang' you'd found in your bin, you had to read the accompanying leaflet complete with hundreds of 'trashies' and their names e.g. STINKY SODA, PUKE POD, YUCKY YOGURT. Harris spent hours reading them, using his fledgling phonics skills, and drawing and writing their names. We ended up covering the whole of the upstairs landing in paper so that he could draw and write a complete gallery of 'garbage'.

Some children will come to school well on their way to beginning to read; books and stories are part of their home landscape. Some children on the other hand, won't even own a book and will never have been read to.

It's important that we don't wait for these children to 'show an interest' in books and reading—it's just not on their radar—reading has never had anything to do with them. As teachers it's up to us to 'backfill' what they've been missing out on and to introduce the wonders of reading and the joy of story—it should never be left to free-choice or a chance encounter. We need to cultivate a reading culture and in the school library and in the classroom we need to provide a wide range of high quality engaging texts—including those which will entice and tempt the most reluctant readers.

As teachers, while we may wish to foster a love of reading, it is important to recognise that not everyone will come to 'love' it, in the same way that not everyone loves sport, cooking or sudoku. Some of our young 'customers' may be more motivated by the 'hard cash value' of knowledge—of being smarter and just knowing stuff—that reading can offer.

Finally, we must accept that while motivation and engagement are important, they are entirely insufficient on their own because—**you can't read for pleasure or learning if reading is a chore, or if you can't actually read.**

## 2. MEANING

What do the words say? What do they mean? The whole point of reading is to understand the writer's message. Ultimately, comprehension depends on our knowledge, of both the words on the page, and the subject in question.

Imagine I have three articles for you to read and answer questions about on the following topics:
*The Decline and Fall of the Roman Empire,*
*Our Universe: A Study of Space and Time* and
*Eastenders: The First Ten Years.*

Your comprehension of these texts, to a large extent, would be dependent on your prior knowledge and, as a result, you're going to find some of these subjects easier than others.

## NURSERY RHYMES, TRADITIONAL TALES AND CULTURAL CAPITAL

Did you know that nursery rhymes have been around for over 270 years? It's a sad fact that many children today are unaware of these childhood rites of passage.

Tommy Thumb's Song Book is the earliest known collection of British nursery rhymes and it was printed back in 1744. It includes many favourites that you will recognise: Baby Bunting, Pat-a-Cake, and London Bridge.

We must backfill these fun pieces of social history that not only tune our children into the sounds and patterns of language—but they are also important for knowledge too or—cultural capital. These tales and rhymes are referenced throughout literature, without an awareness of them, children will be at a disadvantage.

Start every Monday with a different nursery rhyme. Go through it once together, then chant it as a class during any 'wasted' moments such as getting changed for gym or marching to assembly or lunch. Spend the last ten minutes of every Friday afternoon reading a short fairy tale or traditional tale—no need to dissect and discuss—let the story do its own work.

BABY ON THE TREE TOP

Hushaby baby
On the tree top;
When the wind blows
The cradle will rock;
When the bough breaks
The cradle will fall,
Down tumbles baby,
The cradle and all.

As educators it is our duty to develop children's general knowledge through our teaching, ensuring that we have a focus on content as well as skills, and through the reading materials that we provide in class, in particular for study. In many primary classrooms, non-fiction is the poor relative to fiction—but as non-fiction is where we get our knowledge about the world, we have to ensure that it is always 'on the table'. (Although our focus here is on the classroom and reading, it's important to remember that knowledge of the world also accumulates through real life experiences such as school trips, museum visits, and daily life.)

Knowledge of vocabulary is also crucial. When children read a word automatically or whether they sound it out and blend it, if that word is already in their brain, then they will have instant understanding. So, the more words you know, or the more words you have stored in your brain, the better.

There are many ways that we can help children acquire a rich oral vocabulary.

We need to model and take part in high quality listening and talking, showing vocabulary in action as we speak in full, correct sentences, using varied language and words e.g. supplying synonyms alongside words that may be less well-known to aid understanding.

We can teach new words explicitly, either in a planned way as part of using a vocabulary building programme, or in a spontaneous way as new words crop up in the classroom: we discuss them, explore their meanings, spellings, word origins (etymology) and word structures (morphology) e.g. root words, prefixes, suffixes, as well as 'adopting' them and encouraging their use in our speech and writing.

On their own however, these methods are insufficient. **By far the best and easiest way to discover and retain new words is through reading itself**, in conjunction with the techniques described above. Reading provides vocabulary that goes far beyond the level of what we find in ordinary, daily speech; the opportunities to encounter and absorb new words in a meaningful context, while reading, are vast and invaluable.

For many children, especially those who may be experiencing difficulty due to impoverished language, **it is reading that offers both knowledge and words in sufficient quantities to make a difference to their comprehension**. It is therefore essential that all children can readily read and decode new words, to increase their vocabulary and enhance their understanding—in short they need to have mastered the mechanics.

"The limits of my language are the limits of my mind. All I know is what I have words for."

LUDWIG WITTGENSTEIN

# RECIPE for a READER
## The #yuMMMy Ingredients

### 1. Motivation

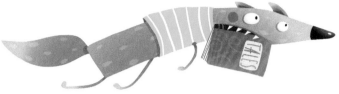

Songs, rhymes, stories and books are essential from birth onwards! Daily sharing of books encourages a love of language and a curiosity about words and the world around us. Listening to and discussing stories improves children's vocabularies, their empathy for others, and fires their imaginations. (If children are reluctant readers, it is often because they are experiencing difficulty with the mechanics of reading, the meaning of what they're reading—or both.)

### 2. Meaning

What does it mean? What do the words say? The whole point of reading is to understand the writer's message. Ultimately, comprehension depends on our knowledge, of both the words on the page, and the subject in question. Developing children's general knowledge and a rich oral vocabulary is essential—and of course, reading, along with high quality listening and talking, is the easiest way to improve both of these!

### 3. Mechanics

To be confident, fluent, motivated readers, children need to read or 'decode' text accurately and 'lift the words off the page' easily. Current international research shows that the most effective way to teach all children to read, write and spell (including strugglers and those with dyslexia) is through rigorous Systematic Synthetic Phonics. This can be taught in daily, fun, fit-for-purpose sessions from 5 years old. For best results, and to enable children to apply their skills and experience success, decodable reading books and materials should be used within a rich and varied literacy environment.

**Being literate unlocks learning and reading for pleasure; the benefits of reading last a lifetime.**

## 3. MECHANICS

The third 'M' is for 'mechanics'. To be confident, fluent, motivated readers, children need to read or 'decode' text accurately and 'lift the words off the page' easily. This is the missing piece of the jigsaw for many children, and while most schools are providing plenty of engagement and opportunities for comprehension—it is often the case that actual teaching of the mechanics of reading is lacking in some way.

There are multiple contributing factors to this scenario, including: a lack of professional knowledge of the pedagogy of reading; a lack of suitable resources that are fit for purpose; initial teacher education that focuses on engagement and comprehension at the expense of giving student teachers instruction in the latest evidence-based classroom practices; and the current prevalent progressive ideology that favours a constructivist or enquiry-based approach to learning, rather than systematic, explicit instruction.

Current international research shows that the most effective way to teach all children to read, write and spell (including strugglers and those diagnosed with dyslexia) is through rigorous Systematic Synthetic Phonics—or SSP.
SSP can be taught in daily, fun, fit-for-purpose sessions from 5 years old. For best results, and to enable children to apply their skills and experience success, decodable reading books and materials should be used within a rich and varied literacy environment.

Without this fundamental teaching in the alphabetic code or how the relationship between the sounds and letters of the English language, reading becomes an *unproductive hack through a forest* for many children—but it doesn't need to be. If children are reluctant readers, it is often because they are experiencing difficulty with the mechanics of reading, the meaning of what they're reading—or both. If reading is slow and stilted, and decoding is laborious then all brain power is being devoted to that task—there is no room left to consider what the text is about or what might happen next. It is only when children achieve automaticity that brain power can then be freed up to focus on meaning and understanding. ***Good decoding is a prerequisite to comprehending: better decoders are better comprehenders.*** We should aim for automaticity in the mechanics—children need enough practice to become fluent readers—they also need sufficient practice to build stamina—so that reading is effortless and automatic.

## "It cannot be left to chance, or for children to ferret out, on their own, how the alphabetic code works."

## SIR JIM ROSE

### INDEPENDENT REVIEW OF THE TEACHING OF EARLY READING

NOTE: A printable copy of the Effective Reading Instruction Checklist on the opposite page is available to download to complete and discuss as a staff.

# EFFECTIVE READING INSTRUCTION CHECKLIST

Our aim is to teach 100% of our children to read, confidently, fluently and independently. ☐

Both elements of reading: decoding (phonics) and comprehension are adequately addressed in our policies and teaching. ☐

We have a high quality phonics programme in place from P1/YR which also provides opportunities for teaching phonics (including phonemic awareness), vocabulary, fluency, comprehension and grammar. ☐

All of our teachers have been trained in phonics, regardless of which age/stage they work with. ☐

We teach the alphabetic code—the sounds/phonemes in our language and their corresponding letter/letters (spelling alternatives). We use alphabetic code charts or sound charts to support teaching and learning. ☐

We teach the skills of reading, writing and spelling including the sub-skills of decoding and blending for reading, oral segmenting and encoding for spelling, and handwriting. ☐

In the early years, we avoid premature grouping and differentiation, and instead focus on 'keeping up' rather than 'catching up'. We provide extra support and 'little and often' practice for slower to learn children. ☐

The only strategy we teach children is phonics 'all-the-way-through-the-word' for reading and for spelling. ☐

We no longer use any of the following: sight words, letter names, miscue analysis, multi-cueing or guessing ☐

Children have opportunities to work independently and at their own pace, using paper-based resources as they practise reading, writing and spelling. (Materials for this should be provided with your phonics programme.) ☐

Decodable reading materials are used for teaching in the early stages. Sentences, texts and reading books follow the phonics being taught and enable children to read independently and make rapid progress. ☐

Regardless of age/stage children throughout the school that are struggling with reading are given appropriate reading instruction and teaching, using a high quality phonics programme as an intervention. ☐

We have a stock of decodable reading books suitable for older learners and which are used throughout the school as appropriate. ☐

Phonics teaching continues up to the end of P7/Y6 for spelling. ☐

We have shared the school's approach to teaching reading with parents—and give clear and explicit advice about how they can best support their child, including an emphasis on reading to, and talking with, their children. ☐

Our classroom practice is fit for purpose. It focuses on the precise and necessary knowledge and skills required for reading. We are careful not to 'lose the learning' in the quest for engagement or active learning. Learning to read is a very real, exciting and fulfilling journey all by itself. ☐

All of the above takes place within a rich literacy environment that instils an appreciation/love of texts and reading in all its forms—whether for pleasure, leisure or learning. ☐

## EFFECTIVE READING INSTRUCTION

It is beyond the scope of this book to provide comprehensive information about beginning reading instruction. But I hope that the contents of this chapter so far have highlighted the importance of decoding when it comes to comprehension—and that the information which follows gives you and your school a 'starter for ten' to evaluate your current practice and hopefully look further into the issue.

A sample reading policy document is also provided—this is available to download. Please feel free to use and adapt to suit your own school.

For those interested, I wasn't always a phonics advocate. You can read about my personal journey and my discovery of the importance of phonics in the appendix. I realised once I started training teachers in the *Reflective Reading* approach that I had a huge professional development need: I didn't know how to teach reading properly, from the beginning. For me, training in phonics was the missing piece of my jigsaw and I wish I'd discovered it years ago. I urge you to read the research and explore this aspect of reading in more detail.

## SYNTHETIC PHONICS PROGRAMMES

Systematic synthetic phonics programmes provide a framework, resources and a rationale for teaching of the alphabetic code (the sounds and the letters) along with word, sentence and text level materials to enable children to practise the skills and sub-skills of reading (decoding, sounding out and blending), writing and spelling.

As well as being research-informed, the following programmes were self-assessed and reviewed against the DfE's core criteria for effective systematic synthetic phonics teaching (Department for Education, England) and are a good place to begin when looking for a suitable programme or phonics training for your school.

### Floppy's Phonics Sounds and Letters
www.floppysphonics.com

### Jolly Phonics
www.jollylearning.co.uk
@jollylearning

### Phonics International
www.phonicsinternational.com
@debbiehepp

### Read Write Inc.
www.ruthmiskin.com
@RuthMiskinEdu

### Sound Discovery
www.syntheticphonics.net

### Sounds Write
www.sounds-write.co.uk
www.theliteracyblog.co.uk/
@SWLiteracy

Note: this list is not exhaustive. Buying into a phonics programme is best accompanied by an investment in training so all teachers know how to use the programme effectively and the principles behind it.

## FURTHER READING ON PHONICS

***Early Reading Instruction: What Science Really Tells Us about How to Teach Reading,*** Diane McGuinness

***Why Our Children Can't Read and What We Can Do About It: A Scientific Revolution in Reading,*** Diane McGuinness (An oldie but goodie, available v.cheaply on Amazon second-hand)

***Phonics and the Resistance to Reading,*** Mike Lloyd-Jones @PhonicsBlog

***Independent Review of the Teaching of Early Reading,*** Jim Rose (Final Report 2006)

Further suggestions are provided in the appendix.

## ESSENTIAL WEBSITES

These websites provide further reading and are a good place to start as the information is free and easily accessible.

**www.dyslexics.org.uk**
Susan Godsland's award-winning site about dyslexia and learning to read, write and spell @SusanGodsland

**www.iferi.org**
International Foundation for Effective Reading Instruction, evidence, resources and forum @IFERIorg

**www.rrf.org.uk**
The Reading Reform Foundation—research, articles and forum @ReadingReform

**www.phonicsinternational.com**
Free resources, assessments and forum @debbiehepp

## DECODABLE BOOKS

All of the main educational publishers now offer phonically decodable strands as part of their reading book schemes.

I also recommend the following:

**www.phonicbooks.co.uk**
Appealing books for every stage and level; chapter books are particularly 'boy-friendly' and suitable for older readers. @phonicbooks

**www.piperbooks.co.uk**
A super range for children that are really struggling or have ASN. (Their Mature Reading Instruction also includes phonically decodable Shakespeare!) @PiperBooks

**www.risingstars-uk.com**
*Reading Planet Rocket Phonics* from Rising Stars is a new range* of varied (fiction & non-fiction) fun and lively readers. @risingstarsedu
*Disclaimer: I wrote 9 of these.

## ALPHABETIC CODE CHARTS

When I first came across Debbie Hepplewhite's Alphabetic Code Chart I had a major light-bulb moment—it's like the times tables for English! I believe ACCs should be on every classroom wall, table and book-bag to support reading and spelling.

They are free to download here, and you'll find big ones, small ones, ones with pictures and without, there's even one that includes teaching notes which I highly recommend:

**www.alphabeticcodecharts.com**

# The English Alphabetic Code

| sounds | simple code | complex code | graphemes, or spelling alternatives, which are code for the sounds | | | | | |
|---|---|---|---|---|---|---|---|---|
| /s/ | s<br>snake | -ss<br>glass | -ce<br>palace | -se<br>house | c (e i y)<br>city | sc<br>scissors | -st-<br>castle | ps<br>pseudonym |
| /a/ | a<br>apple | | | | | | | |
| /t/ | t<br>tent | -tt<br>letter | -ed<br>skipped | | | | | |
| /i/ | i<br>insect | -y<br>cymbals | | | | | | |
| /p/ | p<br>pan | -pp<br>puppet | | | | | | |
| /n/ | n<br>net | -nn<br>bonnet | kn<br>knot | gn<br>gnome | -ne<br>engine | | | |
| /k/ | k<br>kit | c<br>cat | -ck<br>duck | ch<br>chameleon | qu<br>bouquet | que<br>plaque | | |
| /e/ | e<br>egg | -ea<br>head | -ai<br>said | | | | | |
| /h/ | h<br>hat | wh<br>who ? | | | | | | |
| /r/ | r<br>rat | -rr<br>arrow | wr<br>write | rh<br>rhinoceros | | | | |
| /m/ | m<br>map | -mm<br>hammer | -me<br>welcome | -mb<br>thumb | -mn<br>columns | | | |
| /d/ | d<br>dig | -dd<br>puddle | -ed<br>rained | | | | | |
| /g/ | g<br>girl | -gg<br>juggle | gu<br>guitar | gh<br>ghost | -gue<br>catalogue | | | |
| /o/ | o<br>octopus | wa<br>watch | qua<br>qualify | alt<br>salt | | | | |
| /u/ | u<br>umbrella | o<br>son | -ou<br>touch | -ough<br>thoroughfare | | | | |
| /l/ | l<br>ladder | -ll<br>shell | | | | | | |
| /ul/ | -le<br>kettle | -il<br>pencil | -al<br>hospital | -el<br>camel | | | | |
| /f/ | f<br>feathers | -ff<br>cliff | ph<br>photograph | -gh<br>laugh | | | | |
| /b/ | b<br>bat | -bb<br>rabbit | bu<br>building | | | | | |
| /j/ | j<br>jug | -ge<br>cabbage | g (e i y)<br>giraffe | -dge<br>fridge | | | | |
| /y/ | y<br>yawn | | | | | | | |
| /ai/ | ai<br>first aid | -ay<br>tray | a<br>table | -ae<br>sundae | a-e<br>cakes | | | |
|  | -ey<br>prey | -ea<br>break | eigh<br>eight | -aigh<br>straight | | | | |
| /w/ | w<br>web | wh<br>wheel | -u<br>penguin | | | | | |

Copyright Phonics International Ltd 2012

| sounds | simple code | complex code | | | | | |
|---|---|---|---|---|---|---|---|
| /oa/ | oa — oak | ow — bow | o — yo-yo | -oe — oboe | o-e — rope | -ough — dough | eau — plateau |
| /igh/ | -igh — night | -ie — tie | i — behind | -y — fly | i-e — bike | ei — eider duck | eye — eye |
| /ee/ | ee — eel | ea — eat | e — emu | e-e — concrete | -ey — key | -ie — chief | -ine — sardines |
| /i-ee/ | -y — sunny | -ey — monkey | -ie — movie | | | | |
| /or/ | or — fork | oar — oars | -oor — door | ore — snore | -our — four | war — wardrobe | quar — quarter | wa — water |
| | aw — dawn | au — sauce | -al — chalk | -augh — caught | ough — thought | | |
| /z/ | z — zebra | -zz — jazz | -s — fries | -se — cheese | -ze — breeze | | |
| /ng/ | -ng — gong | -n — jungle | | /ngk/ | -nk — ink | -nc — uncle | |
| /v/ | v — violin | -ve — dove | | | | | |
| short /oo/ | -oo — book | -oul — should | -u — push | | | | |
| long /oo/ | oo — moon | -ue — blue | u-e — flute | -ew — crew | -ui — fruit | -ou — soup | -o — move | -ough — through |
| /ks/ | -x — fox | -ks — books | -cks — ducks | -kes — cakes | /gz/ | -x — exam | -gs — pegs |
| /ch/ | ch — chairs | -tch — patch | | /chu/ | -ture — picture | | |
| /sh/ | sh — sheep | ch — chef | -ti — station | -ci — magician | -ssi — admission | | |
| unvoiced /th/ | th — thistle | | voiced /th/ | th — there | | | |
| /kw/ | qu — queen | | | | | | |
| /ou/ | ou — ouch | ow — owl | -ough — plough | | | | |
| /oi/ | oi — ointment | oy — toy | | | | | |
| /yoo/ | -ue — statue | u — unicorn | u-e — tube | ew — new | eu — pneumatic | | |
| /er/ | er — mermaid | ir — birthday | ur — nurse | ear — earth | wor — world | | |
| schwa /er/ 'uh' | -er — mixer | -our — humour | -re — theatre | -ar — collar | -or — sailor | | |
| /ar/ | ar — artist | a — father | alm — palm | -alf — half | -alves — calves | | |
| /air/ | air — hair | -are — hare | -ear — bear | -ere — where | | | |
| /eer/ | eer — deer | ear — ears | -ere — adhere | -ier — cashier | | | |
| /zh/ | -si — television | -s — treasure | -z — azure | g — courgette | -ge — collage | | |

This chart is not definitive. You may discover further code.

Grey dashes indicate that the particular letter/s-sound correspondence is unlikely to begin a word.

Hollow letters alert the reader to various possible pronunciations.

by Debbie Hepplewhite

**The complexities of the English Alphabetic Code:**
1. one sound (phoneme) can be represented by one, two, three or four letters: e.g. /a/ a, /f/ ph, /igh/ igh, /oa/ ough
2. one sound can be represented by multiple spelling alternatives (graphemes): e.g. /oa/: o, oa, ow, oe, o-e, eau, ough
3. one grapheme can represent multiple sounds: e.g. 'ough': /oa/ though, /or/ thought, /oo/ through, /ou/ plough, /u/ thorough

Copyright Phonics International Ltd 2012

## EARLY READING INSTRUCTION AND SYSTEMATIC SYNTHETIC PHONICS: A SAMPLE POLICY

In Primary 1-3 (YR-Y2) a large part of the daily timetable is devoted to teaching children how to read, write and spell. English is a complex language, and as such, it takes around three years to sufficiently master the basics. In line with current international research, we use systematic synthetic phonics in our school, as this has been shown to be the most effective way to teach all children to read and spell—regardless of background or individual difficulties. There is a mounting body of evidence which also shows that this approach is most effective for disadvantaged children and, when taught properly, it can close the attainment gap.

The English language is built out of sounds—or phonemes. Through systematic synthetic phonics children are taught how to blend (synthesise) sounds together to decode words. In addition, this same knowledge is used for spelling—or encoding.
Children are taught about the alphabetic code—and the relationships between the sounds and the letters/spellings (or the grapheme/phoneme correspondences or GPCs). They then use this knowledge when learning the core skills of reading, writing and spelling.

In Primary 1-3 (YR-Y2) we use the programme **<<*insert as appropriate*>>**, on at least four days out of five. Two sounds/letters are introduced per week:

**Monday:** re-cap/review previous learning then teach/introduce new sound/letter and give individual word level practice (reading, writing and spelling)
**Tuesday:** continue to reinforce/apply/practise new sound at sentence level and text level (reading, writing and spelling)
**Wednesday:** re-cap/review previous learning then teach/introduce new sound/letter and give individual word level practice (reading, writing and spelling)
**Thursday:** continue to reinforce/apply/practise new sound at sentence level and text level (reading, writing and spelling)

In all lessons reading, writing and spelling are practised at the same time—with word level, sentence level and text level work taking place—to ensure that children have plenty of practice in applying their knowledge and skills. Sentences and texts are cumulatively decodable, reinforcing previous learning and allowing focussed practice of the new sound/ letter correspondence that has been taught. It is this individual, independent application of skills and knowledge that will secure progress for everyone.

The lesson outlines described above are focussed on enabling children to read, write and spell—but they are also rich, core learning experiences and provide extensive opportunities for comprehension, discussion, the teaching of grammar, and crucially, vocabulary enrichment.

Reading books are also used to support this learning in the classroom and at home. Phonically decodable reading books provide positive reading experiences for children— they use the sounds/letters that children already know and will mean they can read these books independently and with confidence.

By the end of P3 (Y2), if following the pace and practice recommended above, our children will have covered a comprehensive alphabetic code for reading and for spelling; many of the children will almost be totally free readers.

It is important however, that instruction in the alphabetic code continues into P4 (Y3)—and right up until children leave primary school to ensure that the more complex letter/sound correspondences are covered, for spelling in particular.

## SIGHT WORDS

Parents and teachers may at first be surprised to find that we no longer use sight words to teach words to children. This practice has been embedded in **<<*insert country as appropriate*>>** for many decades—and indeed still exists in many schools. However, there is robust research and evidence to show that teaching children to memorise words as a whole, by their shape, is ineffective, and in many cases, detrimental for the teaching of early reading. Reading by sight words is simply memorisation, it is not real reading —and crucially, does not enable children to read any word they may come across. In addition, reading words by sight is a limited strategy—it only works while the reading books and materials used use the words taught to date. If children encounter new or more challenging words—having never learnt it as a sight word—they are left with one ineffective strategy—to guess.

The only strategy that children need, that will work for them every time, is phonics 'all-the-way-through-the-word' for reading and for spelling.

## LETTER NAMES

Often one of the very first things that parents try to teach their children at home is their 'ABCs'—where children sing or chant the letters of the alphabet. However, the names of the letters (Ay, Bee, See etc.) actually have nothing to do with learning to read—as it is the sounds associated with the letters that is important (/a/, /b/, /c/). For this reason, we teach the letter names separately from the alphabetic code—and only once children have a secure basic knowledge of phonics. This avoids confusion at the earliest stages.

## STRUGGLING READERS

There are many reasons why children may struggle with reading. But it must be remembered that, when research-informed, effective reading instruction is used, it is entirely possible to teach every child to read. It will only be in 2%-3% cases, where children have profound difficulties or disabilities, that they may be unable to reach the desired level of literacy. Even children, who may previously have been described as dyslexic, can be taught to read.

From Primary 1 (YR) it is crucial that slower to learn children are given sufficient time to learn—and this will usually mean more little and often practice—to ensure that these children can keep up with the work of the class, rather than allowing them to fall behind and be in the impossible situation of 'catching up' with their peers.

It is not necessary to buy or use specific intervention programmes for struggling readers. If you buy a high quality phonics programme this should also be used for intervention purposes.

## RESOURCES

The methodology we use at **<<insert school name>>** is systematic synthetic phonics and we follow its principles for the teaching of reading. We use the following resources to support the teaching and learning of reading in the classroom:

**<<insert as appropriate>>**: a phonics and intervention programme—and a spelling programme throughout the school

**<<insert as appropriate>>**: phonically decodable reading books

**<<insert as appropriate>>**: we use these books with children who have ASN or who are experiencing difficulties with reading

**Alphabetic Code Charts**: these are used throughout the school, in every classroom and in book bags. They support teaching and learning in reading—and also help children become independent, accurate spellers.

## RED HERRINGS AND WHITE ELEPHANTS

Unfortunately, within the world of reading instruction there are still some unhelpful, misguided, or simply outdated, practices and ideas that, despite research and evidence-based practice, refuse to disappear. At best these strategies waste valuable instruction time, but at worst they can confuse struggling learners, compounding problems and hindering progress. Beware!

## THE MYSTERY OF MULTI-CUEING

This white elephant goes under several different names—or disguises: **multi-cueing, three-cueing, Searchlights**, and the **three-domain model.** Although it's been around since the 1970s, and should really have stayed there, multi-cueing is still being used in schools and being promoted in teacher education, along with useless, outdated practices such as miscue analysis and *Reading Recovery*.

The method purports that readers need to attend to the following cues, in order of importance:

**semantic** (meaning),
**syntactic** (structure and grammar) and
**grapho-phonic** (how words look and sound).

More often than not, this approach relies on guessing:

- guessing what a word might be
- skipping a word, reading on, and then guessing
- skipping a word altogether and relying on the 'gist'
- guessing a word from its initial letter or sound
- using the picture* to guess what a word might be

In brief, guessing of any kind should not be considered a valid strategy. When taught through phonics, there is no need to guess at all. Children simply use their phonic knowledge '***all-the-way-through-the-word'*** to decode it and lift it off the page. This produces readers who approach text from a position of knowledge—they are fearless when they meet new words as they can apply their phonic knowledge instead of having to grapple with the unknown and resort to hazarding a guess.

(*pictures of course enhance our reading and certainly add to our context knowledge—but they should never be used as a tool to guess individual words)

## A DEVELOPMENTAL APPROACH

In schools we sometimes talk of a developmental approach or *'developmentally appropriate practice'.* Often, we expect reading and writing to appear… *as if by magic*.

We talk about *'emergent writing'*—and are excited when children make squiggles to please us that look like letters. It can feel like a mini miracle… and it usually is, as no-one will even have shown the child in question how to hold a pencil or form their letters.

Some children take to reading effortlessly.

A select few—usually those that have the support at home—are the ones who start reading by osmosis. Often, they have learned to read on the lap of their parents; they've had the rhymes, the repetition, and a bedtime story every night.

However, for the rest, reading and writing will not appear magically; we need to teach them about letters and sounds and how they work. Reading is not a natural phenomenon; there is no magical developmental milestone that we need to wait for.

Once children start school it is imperative that they learn to read. While our intentions may be good, we should never withhold essential teaching from those that need it the most, under the misapprehension that they are 'not ready'. Every day that we delay the teaching of reading, the gap between our least able and most able learners is getting bigger all the time.

Billy might not know his nursery rhymes or show signs of phonemic awareness, but while he is digging for worms in the mud, or putting picture cards into the right order, Lorna is reading about the life cycle of butterflies in the book corner and having a discussion about it with the teacher. The cumulative effect of all of this on her vocabulary, knowledge and skills is mind-blowing.

For Billy, and for our other disadvantaged children, teaching them to read is the single most significant thing we can do for their education, now and in the future.

Being literate is literally the best chance they've got.

CHAPTER 3

# Planning, Tracking and Assessment

## PLANNING OVERVIEW

In this chapter we'll take a brief look at the materials available within *Reflective Reading* for planning, tracking and assessment; these fall under three headings and I'll explain each in turn:

- **Reflective Reading Teacher Tracker**
- **Child Friendly Assessment Booklets**
- **Literacy and English Benchmarks**
- **THE BIGGER PICTURE**

## PLANNING USING THE TEACHER TRACKER

The full Teacher Tracker is provided over the next few pages and it is also available in the digital download. It is designed to be an easy way to keep track of planning for reading in the classroom; while providing an overview of the reading outcomes covered over the course of each term and a full school year.

The tracker uses the *Experiences and Outcomes* from Scotland's *Curriculum for Excellence* as a basis for creating 'reading focus' statements, but these are general enough to be useful wherever you are teaching and you may wish to add to or adapt some of these to reflect your curriculum more closely.

The planner is organised by the *Curriculum for Excellence* levels: *Early, First, Second* and *Third* and by the subdivisions: *Enjoyment and choice, Tools for reading, Finding and using information, and Understanding, analysing, evaluating.* The levels relate to the following year groups:

**Early Level:** Nursery/Primary 1; Nursery/YR
**First Level:** Primary 2-Primary 4; Y1-Y3
**Second Level:** Primary 5-Primary 7; Y4-Y6
**Third Level:** Primary 7-Third Year (Secondary school); Year 6-Year 9

It is important to note that, depending on progress and needs, some children may start learning at these levels earlier or later than their peers. For example, once children begin a high quality phonics programme in P1/YR, they will already be working beyond Early Level and will be well into working at First Level; it is perhaps helpful to think of the levels as minimum requirements. Third Level is also included in the tracker as some children may already be learning at this level while in P7/Y6.

As explained in the previous chapter, it is unhelpful and may indeed be damaging to group children by ability, especially in the earliest stages. Wherever possible, I would recommend whole class teaching for basic skills in English and maths in particular, which includes direct teaching and individual practice. I'll talk more about grouping in later chapters.

The tracker is designed so that each level may be printed onto a single sheet of A4 paper (landscape orientation), if desired. In this way, it provides an 'at-a-glance' handy planning document, where you can see your whole year of planning for reading at once.

You will notice that beside each statement there are four boxes—this is one box per term. When planning, simply highlight the boxes next to the statements that you hope to address during teaching and learning for that term. During, or at the end of the term, you can then 'tick', 'dot' or leave the box blank depending on how well you feel the requirements of the statement have been covered and understood. More practice may be required and you may wish to highlight it again for the next term.

Some of the statements are easy to tick, as they will be covered naturally most days in class. Others, especially the ones included in the *Understanding, analysing and evaluating* section are more difficult, as they concern higher order thinking skills; but these are the ones we are really going to focus on during *Reflective Reading* so that you can be sure they are being covered.

By tracking the statements in this way, it will become clear where there are 'gaps' that need to be filled or particular areas that require reinforcement. As the levels span years, this

document will become a useful tool to pass on to subsequent teachers to inform planning and 'next steps' and to ensure balanced coverage of all of the reading outcomes.

This document is for the teacher, it is not designed to be used as an 'assessment' or 'tick sheet' for individual children. (This would be a huge waste of precious time.) Depending on the needs of the class, you may decide to print an A4 overview for each reading group, especially if they are working on different levels. However, where this is the case, minimise work for yourself and highlight similar statements for both groups e.g. if you have a group working at Second Level who have a reading focus on the statement *'I make notes on what I have read, watched, or listened to, choosing appropriate headings'* highlight the same/equivalent statement for your First Level group. **This will allow whole class teaching, modelling and discussion where appropriate.**

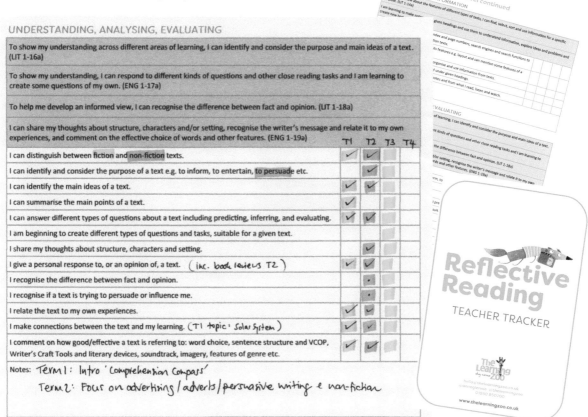

# Reflective Reading: Early Level

## ENJOYMENT AND CHOICE

| | | | | |
|---|---|---|---|---|
| I enjoy exploring and playing with the patterns and sounds of language and can use what I learn. (LIT 0-01a, LIT 0-21a, LIT 0-20a) | | | | |
| I enjoy exploring and choosing stories and other texts to watch, read or listen to, and can share my likes and dislikes. (LIT 0-01b, LIT 0-21a, LIT 0-11b) | | | | |
| I enjoy listening to rhymes, songs and stories and being read to. | | | | |
| I enjoy watching and listening to television programmes, films and audio books/stories/songs/CDs. | | | | |
| I recognise language patterns and join in with familiar, repeated rhymes and stories. | | | | |
| I choose my own texts, and attempt to 'read' independently. | | | | |
| I handle books appropriately e.g. right way up, 'read' left to right, and turn pages carefully. | | | | |
| I say what I like/don't like about a story or text I know. | | | | |

## TOOLS FOR READING

| | | | | |
|---|---|---|---|---|
| I explore sounds, letters and words, discovering how they work together, and I can use what I learn to help me as I read and write. (ENG 0-12a, LIT 0-13a, LIT 0-21a) | | | | |
| I recognise familiar words and signs both inside and out e.g. my name, logos, environmental print. | | | | |
| I use picture clues to gain meaning from text. | | | | |
| I understand the terms book, cover, beginning, end, page, word, letter, line and sound. | | | | |
| I show an awareness of some sounds of letters of the alphabet e.g. can play I-Spy. | | | | |
| I am beginning to recognise the relationship between printed letters and their corresponding sounds. | | | | |

## FINDING AND USING INFORMATION

| | | | | |
|---|---|---|---|---|
| I use signs, books or other texts to find useful or interesting information and I use this to plan, make choices or learn new things. (LIT 0-14a) | | | | |
| I am becoming aware of texts, books, computers and the internet as sources of information. | | | | |
| I can sequence pictures of known stories and texts and can invent stories and texts to match pictures. | | | | |
| I am learning, by observing and doing, how to find information in different types of texts e.g. using pictures, search engines, contents, index, page numbers etc. | | | | |

## UNDERSTANDING, ANALYSING, EVALUATING

| | | | | |
|---|---|---|---|---|
| To help me understand stories and other texts, I ask questions and link what I am learning with what I already know. (LIT 0-07a, LIT 0-16a, ENG 0-17a) | | | | |
| I enjoy exploring events and characters in stories and other texts, sharing my thoughts in different ways. (LIT 0-19a) | | | | |
| I can retell events in a story or information from a non-fiction text. (may be brief) | | | | |
| I am curious about what I am reading, listening to or watching. I can answer and ask questions about it. | | | | |
| I make predictions about what might happen next. | | | | |
| I can say what I already know about a subject or story. | | | | |
| I can talk about characters or my 'favourite bits' of a text or story and explain why I like them. | | | | |

Notes:

# Reflective Reading: First Level

## ENJOYMENT AND CHOICE

| I regularly select and read, listen to or watch texts which I enjoy and find interesting, and I can explain why I prefer certain texts and authors. (LIT 1-11a) | | | | |
|---|---|---|---|---|
| I enjoy being read to and like listening and responding to jokes, poems, rhymes, songs and stories. | | | | |
| I enjoy watching and listening to television programmes, films, clips and audio CDs. | | | | |
| I use the covers, pictures, blurbs, titles and text to help me make reading choices. | | | | |
| I regularly choose my own texts, in school and at home, to read for pleasure e.g. jokes, comics, picture books, stories, novels, short stories, poems and games etc. | | | | |
| I regularly choose my own texts, in school and at home, to read for information e.g. websites, apps, encyclopaedias, non-fiction books, 'How to..' , instruction books, newspapers etc. | | | | |
| I regularly choose my own texts, in school and at home, to watch and listen for pleasure and for information e.g. television programmes, films, podcasts, music, YouTube, games etc. | | | | |
| I can talk about different types of texts and say what types of texts I prefer and why. | | | | |
| I can talk about different authors and their texts, explaining who my favourite author is and why. | | | | |
| Notes: | | | | |

## TOOLS FOR READING

| I can use my knowledge of sight vocabulary, phonics, context clues, punctuation and grammar to read with understanding and expression. (ENG 1-12a) | | | | |
|---|---|---|---|---|
| I am learning to select and use strategies and resources before I read, and as I read, to help make the meaning of texts clear. (LIT 1-13a) | | | | |
| I read confidently and fluently and have achieved an appropriate level of automaticity when reading texts of a suitable level. | | | | |
| I use my phonics 'all-the-way-through-the-word' to sound out and blend unknown words. | | | | |
| I can read a familiar text aloud fluently and unknown texts with increasing fluency. | | | | |
| I use context clues, the blurb and pictures to enhance my understanding of text. | | | | |
| When necessary, I can use a dictionary to clarify my understanding of unknown words. | | | | |
| I can 'read' pictures or films and make meaning from these texts without words. (visual literacy) | | | | |
| I can skim read a text quickly to get the idea of what it is about. | | | | |
| I can scan a text for particular words or information. | | | | |
| I read aloud with understanding, accuracy and expression, paying attention to punctuation: capital letters, full stops, question marks, exclamation marks, commas etc. and text in **bold** and *italics*. | | | | |
| I can sequence pictures of stories and texts and can invent stories and texts to match pictures. | | | | |
| I am developing my skills in finding  information in books and online e.g. using pictures, search engines, contents, index, page numbers etc. | | | | |
| Notes: | | | | |

## Reflective Reading: First Level continued

### FINDING AND USING INFORMATION

| | | | | |
|---|---|---|---|---|
| Using what I know about the features of different types of texts, I can find, select, sort and use information for a specific purpose. (LIT 1-14a) | | | | |
| I am learning to make notes under given headings and use them to understand information, explore ideas and problems and create new texts. (LIT 1-15a) | | | | |
| I can use the contents, alphabetical index and page numbers, search engines and search functions to help me locate information in non-fiction texts. | | | | |
| I can identify a text type from some of its features e.g. layout and can mention some features of a given text type. | | | | |
| I can find, select, sort, highlight, classify, organise and use information from texts. | | | | |
| I am learning to make notes on what I read under given headings. | | | | |
| I am learning to create new texts from my notes and from what I read, listen and watch. | | | | |
| Notes: | | | | |

### UNDERSTANDING, ANALYSING, EVALUATING

| | | | | |
|---|---|---|---|---|
| To show my understanding across different areas of learning, I can identify and consider the purpose and main ideas of a text. (LIT 1-16a) | | | | |
| To show my understanding, I can respond to different kinds of questions and other close reading tasks and I am learning to create some questions of my own. (ENG 1-17a) | | | | |
| To help me develop an informed view, I can recognise the difference between fact and opinion. (LIT 1-18a) | | | | |
| I can share my thoughts about structure, characters and/or setting, recognise the writer's message and relate it to my own experiences, and comment on the effective choice of words and other features. (ENG 1-19a) | | | | |
| I can distinguish between fiction and non-fiction texts. | | | | |
| I can identify and consider the purpose of a text e.g. to inform, to entertain, to persuade etc. | | | | |
| I can identify the main ideas of a text. | | | | |
| I can summarise the main points of a text. | | | | |
| I can answer different types of questions about a text including predicting, inferring, and evaluating. | | | | |
| I am beginning to create different types of questions and tasks, suitable for a given text. | | | | |
| I share my thoughts about structure, characters and setting. | | | | |
| I give a personal response to, or an opinion of, a text. | | | | |
| I recognise the difference between fact and opinion. | | | | |
| I recognise if a text is trying to persuade or influence me. | | | | |
| I relate the text to my own experiences. | | | | |
| I make connections between the text and my learning. | | | | |
| I comment on how good/effective a text is referring to: word choice, sentence structure and VCOP, Writer's Craft Tools and literary devices, soundtrack, imagery, features of genre etc. | | | | |
| Notes:  VCOP = Vocabulary, Connectives, Openers, Punctuation | | | | |

# Reflective Reading: Second Level

## ENJOYMENT AND CHOICE

| I regularly select and read, listen to or watch texts which I enjoy and find interesting, and I can explain why I prefer certain texts and authors. (LIT 2-11a) | | | | |
|---|---|---|---|---|
| I enjoy reading in all forms covering a wide range of texts and text types; I am a reader. | | | | |
| I regularly choose my own texts, in school and at home, to read for pleasure e.g. novels, short stories, comics, magazines, websites, graphic novels, poems, multi-modal texts and games etc. | | | | |
| I regularly choose my own texts, in school and at home, to read for information e.g. websites, apps, encyclopaedias, non-fiction books, 'How to...'/recipe/instruction books, newspapers etc. | | | | |
| I regularly choose my own texts, in school and at home, to read, watch and listen for pleasure and information e.g. TV programmes, films, podcasts, music, YouTube and social media etc. | | | | |
| I choose my own books or texts for study in class. | | | | |
| I can discuss different types of texts and talk about which types of texts I prefer and why. | | | | |
| I can discuss different authors and their texts, explaining who my favourite authors are and why. | | | | |
| Notes: | | | | |

## TOOLS FOR READING

| Through developing my knowledge of context clues, punctuation, grammar and layout, I can read unfamiliar texts with increasing fluency, understanding and expression. (ENG 2-12a) | | | | |
|---|---|---|---|---|
| I can select and use a range of strategies and resources before I read, and as I read, to make meaning clear, and give reasons for my selection. (LIT 2-13a) | | | | |
| I can read a range of level appropriate familiar and unfamiliar texts fluently and accurately. | | | | |
| I read aloud with understanding and expression, paying attention to punctuation, verbs and adverbs e.g. she whispered, 'You mean...' he paused for effect etc. and text in **bold**/*italics*. | | | | |
| I use my knowledge of structure and layout to locate information e.g. introduction, conclusion, paragraphs, headings and sub-headings etc. | | | | |
| I can locate information quickly and effectively by using text marking, ICT resources and search functions, contents and indexes. | | | | |
| I can 'read' pictures or films and make meaning from these texts without words. (visual literacy) | | | | |
| I can skim read to identify the main ideas of a text and I can scan a text for particular words, information or the answer to a question. | | | | |
| I use context clues, punctuation, parts of speech, and root words, prefixes and suffixes to consider new words and to help me read for meaning. | | | | |
| I can use a dictionary and/or a thesaurus, as appropriate, to help me in my work. | | | | |
| I can 'read between the lines' to interpret meaning from actions, dialogue and descriptions. | | | | |
| Notes: | | | | |

# Reflective Reading: Second Level continued

## FINDING AND USING INFORMATION

| | | | | |
|---|---|---|---|---|
| Using what I know about the features of different types of texts, I can find, select, sort information from a variety of sources and use this for different purposes. (LIT 2-14a) | | | | |
| I can make notes, organise them under suitable headings and use them to understand information, develop my thinking, explore problems and create new texts, using my own words as appropriate. (LIT 2-15a) | | | | |
| I can use the contents, alphabetical index and page numbers, search engines and search functions to help me locate information in non-fiction texts. | | | | |
| I can identify a text by its features and can describe in detail the features of a given text type. | | | | |
| I can find, select, sort, highlight, classify, organise & use information from a variety of sources. | | | | |
| I make notes on what I have read, watched, or listened to, choosing appropriate headings. | | | | |
| I create new texts from my notes using my own words as appropriate. (I might quote from the text.) | | | | |
| Notes: | | | | |

## UNDERSTANDING, ANALYSING, EVALUATING

| | | | | |
|---|---|---|---|---|
| To show my understanding across different areas of learning, I can identify and consider the purpose and main ideas of a text and use supporting detail. (LIT 2-16a) | | | | |
| To show my understanding, I can respond to literal, inferential and evaluative questions and other close reading tasks and can create different kinds of questions of my own. (ENG 2-17a) | | | | |
| To help me develop an informed view, I can identify and explain the difference between fact and opinion, recognise when I am being influenced, and have assessed how useful and believable my sources are. (LIT 2-18a) | | | | |
| I can: discuss structure, characterisation and/or setting; recognise the relevance of the writer's theme and how this relates to my own and others' experiences; discuss the writer's style and other features appropriate to genre. (ENG 2-19a) | | | | |
| I can identify and consider the purpose of a text e.g. to inform, to entertain, to persuade etc. | | | | |
| I can identify and summarise the main ideas of a text, using supporting detail. | | | | |
| I can answer different types of questions about a text including predicting, inferring, and evaluating. | | | | |
| I can create different types of questions and tasks, suitable for a given text. | | | | |
| I can identify and explain the difference between fact and opinion and can detect bias. | | | | |
| I recognise if a text is trying to persuade or influence me. | | | | |
| I can assess how useful and believable my sources are. | | | | |
| I share my thoughts about structure, characterisation and setting. | | | | |
| I give a personal response to, or an opinion of, a text. | | | | |
| I recognise the relevance of the writer's theme to my own and others' experiences and the wider world and can make connections between the text and my learning. | | | | |
| I comment on a writer's style and how effective a text is referring to: VCOP, literary devices and features specific to each genre etc. e.g. film: camera angle; soundtrack etc. | | | | |
| Notes: Notes: VCOP = Vocabulary, Connectives, Openers, Punctuation | | | | |

# Reflective Reading: Third Level

## ENJOYMENT AND CHOICE

| | | | | |
|---|---|---|---|---|
| I regularly select and read, listen to or watch texts for enjoyment and interest, and I can express how well they meet my needs and expectations and give reasons, with evidence, for my personal response. I can identify sources to develop the range of my reading. (LIT 3-11a) | | | | |
| I enjoy reading in all forms covering a wide range of texts and text types; I am a reader. | | | | |
| I regularly choose my own texts, in school and at home, to read for pleasure e.g. novels, short stories, comics, magazines, websites, graphic novels, poems, multi-modal texts and games etc. | | | | |
| I regularly choose my own texts, in school and at home, to read for information e.g. websites, apps, encyclopaedias, non-fiction books, 'How to...' /recipe/instruction books, newspapers etc. | | | | |
| I regularly choose my own texts, in school and at home, to read, watch and listen for pleasure and information e.g. TV programmes, films, podcasts, music, YouTube and social media etc. | | | | |
| I can express detailed opinions about texts and authors, giving reasons, backed by evidence, to support my personal response. | | | | |
| I can identify sources to develop the range of my reading e.g. libraries, book shops, online book sellers, reviews, blogs, social media, personal recommendations etc. | | | | |
| Notes: | | | | |

## TOOLS FOR READING

| | | | | |
|---|---|---|---|---|
| Through developing my knowledge of context clues, punctuation, grammar and layout, I can read unfamiliar texts with increasing fluency, understanding and expression. (ENG 3-12a) | | | | |
| I can select and use a range of strategies and resources I find most useful before I read, and as I read, to monitor and check my understanding. (LIT 3-13a) | | | | |
| I can read a range of level appropriate texts fluently and accurately. | | | | |
| I read aloud with understanding and expression, paying attention to punctuation, verbs and adverbs e.g. she whispered, he added cautiously, 'You mean...' he paused for effect etc. | | | | |
| I use my knowledge of structure and layout to locate information e.g. introduction, conclusion, paragraphs, headings and sub-headings etc. | | | | |
| I can locate information quickly and effectively by using skimming and scanning, text marking, ICT resources and search functions, contents and indexes. | | | | |
| I can 'read' pictures or films and make meaning from these texts without words. (visual literacy) | | | | |
| I can skim read to identify the main ideas of a text and I can scan a text for particular words, information or the answer to a question. | | | | |
| I use context clues, punctuation, parts of speech, and root words, prefixes and suffixes to consider new words and to help me read for meaning. | | | | |
| As I read I automatically monitor and check my understanding, re-reading or slowing down as appropriate. | | | | |
| I can 'read between the lines' to interpret meaning from actions, dialogue and descriptions. | | | | |
| Notes: | | | | |

# Reflective Reading: Third Level continued

## FINDING AND USING INFORMATION

| | | | | |
|---|---|---|---|---|
| Using what I know about the features of different types of texts, I can find, select, sort, summarise, link and use information from different sources. (LIT 3-14a) | | | | |
| I can make notes, organise them to develop my thinking, help retain and recall information, explore issues and create new texts, using my own words as appropriate. (LIT 3-15a) | | | | |
| I can describe in detail different text types and their purpose, structure/organisation, language and specific features. | | | | |
| I can find, select, sort, summarise, link and use information from a variety of sources. | | | | |
| I make notes and organise them to develop my thinking and help retain & recall information. | | | | |
| I create new texts from my notes using my own words as appropriate. | | | | |
| Notes: | | | | |

## UNDERSTANDING, ANALYSING, EVALUATING

| | | | | |
|---|---|---|---|---|
| To show my understanding across different areas of learning, I can: identify and consider the purpose, main concerns or concepts and use supporting detail; make inferences from key statements; identify and discuss similarities and differences between different types of text. (LIT 3-16a) | | | | |
| To show my understanding, I can comment, with evidence, on the content and form of short and extended texts, and respond to literal, inferential and evaluative questions and other types of close reading tasks. (ENG 3-17a) | | | | |
| To help me develop an informed view, I am exploring the techniques used to influence my opinion. I can recognise persuasion and assess the reliability of information and credibility and value of my sources. (LIT 3-18a) | | | | |
| I can discuss & evaluate the structure, characterisation &/or setting using some supporting evidence; identify the main theme of the text and recognise the relevance this has to my own & others' experiences; identify & comment on aspects of the writer's style & other features appropriate to genre using some relevant evidence. (ENG 3-19a) | | | | |
| I can identify and consider the purpose, main concerns or concepts of a text & use supporting detail. | | | | |
| I can make inferences from key statements. | | | | |
| I can comment, with evidence, on the content and form of short and extended texts. | | | | |
| I can identify and discuss similarities and differences between different types of texts. | | | | |
| I can respond to literal, inferential and evaluative questions and other close reading tasks. | | | | |
| I can create different types of questions and tasks suitable for a given or chosen text. | | | | |
| I can identify and explain the difference between fact and opinion and can detect bias. | | | | |
| I recognise persuasion and am exploring the techniques used to influence my opinion. | | | | |
| I can assess the reliability of information and credibility and value of my sources. | | | | |
| I can discuss and evaluate the structure, characterisation and/or setting using some supporting evidence from the text. | | | | |
| I can identify the writer's theme and recognise its relevance to my own & others' experiences, and the wider world and can make connections between the text and my learning. | | | | |
| I can identify and comment on aspects of a writer's style (VCOP, literary devices etc.) its effect on the reader and other features specific to genre using some relevant evidence. | | | | |
| Notes: Notes: VCOP = Vocabulary, Connectives, Openers, Punctuation | | | | |

## THE CHILD FRIENDLY ASSESSMENT BOOKLETS

The *Child Friendly Reading Assessments* are designed to be used in conjunction with the other *Reflective Reading* materials, in particular, the *Teacher Tracker* and the *Comprehension Compass* (which we'll meet in Chapter 5: Long Read)

The purpose of the child-friendly assessments is to encourage reflection on reading progress through discussion with peers and with the teacher. When used termly, they can provide valuable conversations, evidence and tracking of achievement in reading over the course of a year.

By involving children as fully as possible in the assessment process it is hoped that, as in *Assessment is for Learning*, they will become more aware of their own strengths, weaknesses, skills and knowledge in all aspects of reading. In this way, coupled with greater clarity in the teaching of reading, using the common language of the statements, modelling specific reading skills and increased discussion surrounding higher order skills and progression in reading, children themselves will eventually be able to identify and describe their own 'learning gaps' and be able to plan and work on their 'next steps'.

As with the *Teacher Tracker*, the *Child Friendly Assessment Booklets* are organised by *Curriculum for Excellence* levels: *Early, First, Second* and *Third* and by the subdivisions: *Enjoyment and choice, Tools for reading, Finding and using information,* and *Understanding, analysing, evaluating.* Each PDF document can be printed double-sided on A4, which can then be folded into a simple booklet. It is suggested that four of these booklets are completed each year; one per child, each term. Depending on the needs of your class, and individual children, you can choose from the booklets below:

* These stages are given as suggestions only. Progression through the levels will be earlier or later for some. The class teacher will be best able to decide which assessment booklet is suitable for the children in their class, and how and when they wish to complete it during the term.

| LEVEL | STAGE* | BOOKLET DESCRIPTION |
|---|---|---|
| Early/First | P1 /P2 (YR/Y1) | Single page. Can be scribed during discussion or drawn on/filled in by child when able. |
| First | P2-P4 (Y1-Y3) | Booklet contains all statements for First Level. Highlight focus statements for discussion. |
| Second | P5-P7 (Y4-Y6) | Booklet contains all statements for Second Level. Highlight focus statements for discussion. |
| Third | P7 (Y6) | Booklet contains all statements for Third Level. Use as required. |

### SELF AND PEER ASSESSMENT

With younger children, depending on the age/stage, they can simply draw pictures in the boxes at first about what they are watching/reading/ listening to. They can chat about and share their drawings with other groups, or as a whole class. Initially, we're only looking for children to express their own opinions about books, reading etc. what they like/ don't like.

When it comes to the statements, the teacher can guide and model for the class: 'Oh, it says here that *I know my letters and sounds and use them to read.*' Do we know all of our letters and sounds? What sounds are we learning this week? Hmm... are we green for go on that? Or are we still learning and practising?'

The assessment should never, at any time, be purely a 'paper exercise' to be filled in. The real value is in class conversations and peer discussions on the 'nitty gritty' of reading progress and of course enjoyment of reading and favourite texts.

There is one box per statement. Children could traffic light statements using coloured pencils (red, orange, green) or they could simply 'tick', 'dot' or 'cross' to indicate their level of confidence. Decisions will be made in consultation with peers and, when appropriate, with the teacher. It will be important to highlight that you can't 'cheat'; the teacher will review each booklet (ideally in consultation with the child) and provide a comment. There is space for a child or parent/carer comment too.

The *Child Friendly Assessment Booklets* provide a springboard for conversations, a 'learning dialogue' and a way of recording

what's being discussed. It should be an enjoyable time, where suddenly, your opinion counts; if you love *The Gruffalo, Beast Quest, Horrible Histories, Rainbow Fairies, Minecraft*—or whatever—you get a chance to share and talk about it. One teacher told me about an enthusiastic girl in her class who kept asking: '*When are we going to talk about our reading again?*' That's the type of engagement we're after! This is also a prime time to work on listening/talking skills including taking turns, being an active listener and asking appropriate questions.

The booklets also give teachers valuable information and insight into children's real feelings about reading, what subjects they are really interested in (which can be used to your advantage in class), how confident they are becoming in the skills of reading and how familiar they are with them. It provides a 'pulling together' —a plenary of sorts and a 'joining the dots' for all the hard work that is going on in reading everyday. (It is also great preparation for the types of questions HMIe ask children during an inspection.)

FULL VERSIONS OF ALL OF THE RESOURCES AND SAMPLES IN THIS CHAPTER ARE AVAILABLE TO DOWNLOAD HERE:

www.thelearningzoo.co.uk/bookstuff

# Me and My Reading

How many stars for reading? ⭐⭐⭐⭐⭐

by

My favourite text is...

I like it because...

What I'm reading at the moment:

What I'm watching / listening to at the moment:

# Reflective Reading

by

**What I'm reading at the moment...**

**What I'm watching and listening to...**

Child Friendly Assessment: First Level

**Things to work on...**

**Comments...**

by:

by:

Marks out of 10 for reading? Circle how you feel!

1   2   3   4   5   6   7   8   9   10

I hate reading          I love reading

## Enjoyment and choice

|  | A lot | A little | Never |
|---|---|---|---|
| I read for pleasure. | | | |
| I choose what I want to read e.g. books, comics etc. | | | |
| I choose what I want to watch / listen to e.g. TV, films | | | |

My favourite texts are...

because...

My favourite authors are...

because...

## Tools for reading

|  |  |  |  |
|---|---|---|---|
| I know my letters and sounds (phonics) and use them for reading. | | | |
| I use my phonics to sound out and blend unknown words. | | | |
| I can use context clues, blurb and pictures to help me understand. | | | |
| I can skim read a text quickly. | | | |
| I can scan a text for particular words or information. | | | |
| I can read aloud with confidence. (Fluency, Accuracy, Speed, Expression) | | | |

## Finding and using information

|  |  |  |  |
|---|---|---|---|
| I can identify a text from some of its features. | | | |
| I can find, select, sort and use information in texts. | | | |
| I can make notes on what I read under suitable headings. | | | |
| I can create new texts from my notes and/ or from what I read, listen and watch. | | | |

## Understanding, analysing and evaluating

|  |  |  |  |
|---|---|---|---|
| I can identify and consider the purpose of a text (e.g. to inform, to entertain, to persuade etc.) | | | |
| I can identify the main ideas of a text. | | | |
| I can summarise the main points of a text. | | | |
| I can answer different types of questions about a text (including predicting, inferring, evaluating) | | | |
| I can create different types of questions and tasks, suitable for a given text. | | | |
| I can share my thoughts about structure, characters and setting. | | | |
| I can give a personal response to, or an opinion of, a text. | | | |
| I can recognise the difference between fact and opinion. | | | |
| I can recognise if a text is trying to persuade / influence me. | | | |
| I can relate the text to my own experiences. | | | |
| I can make connections between the text and my learning. | | | |
| I can comment on how good / effective a text is referring to: word choice, soundtrack, imagery, features of genre etc. | | | |

So, how are you doing? Progress? Things to be proud of?

I think that...

## THE LITERACY AND ENGLISH BENCHMARKS FOR READING

The *Literacy and English Benchmarks* published by Education Scotland are designed to support practitioners' professional judgement as they consider if individual children have achieved a reading level. These should be used in a holistic way, alongside classwork, day-to-day learning, assessments, learning conversations and standardised tests. They are not designed to be 'ticked off', therefore no boxes are provided. The benchmarks are in an A4 format, with one level per page. They are also available in the digital download. More information about the benchmarks and their use is available online.

## IMPORTANT NOTE: TOOLS FOR READING

The benchmarks and statements provided for the '*Tools for Reading*' organiser are problematic, in that they conflict with current international research on reading and systematic synthetic phonics. Alternative/additional statements have been provided below to ensure secure progress and judgements.

It is recommended that teachers have a simple record keeping system in place for tracking children's current knowledge of the alphabetic code. Skills in blending (where children blend sounds together to form words) should also be monitored.

### TOOLS FOR READING (additional statements for Early/First Levels)

• Hears and can 'discern' words when spoken in phonemes e.g. teacher gives the sounds/phonemes only: /c/-/a/-/t/ and the child says 'cat'.
• Hears and can point to/select/or write a letter/grapheme in response to a spoken sound/phoneme e.g. teacher says /t/ or /sh/ and child selects letter/graphemes 't' or 'sh'.
• Hears and can blend phonemes/sounds to form words.
• Knows the difference between a letter/grapheme and a sound/phoneme.
• Finger tracks under letters/letter groups/graphemes while blending sounds/phonemes for reading.*
• Uses knowledge of letter/sound (grapheme/phoneme) correspondences to read words.
• Uses knowledge of phonics to tackle all words, including tricky words, and unknown words.
• Reads aloud and independently texts that are aligned with their current developing phonic knowledge e.g. phonically decodable sentences, texts or reading book during class work.
• Reads aloud/silently and/or independently/with support any text that is of interest using their current developing phonic knowledge e.g. book corner or library books, reading for pleasure etc.

*finger tracking is a transitional tool and may not be required once children achieve automaticity and can read without blending; it will still be useful to support reading of new/unknown words.

N.B. Using a high quality phonics programme, children should be 'free readers' by the end of P3/P4 at the latest and be able to progress to short chapter novels or similar.

## LITERACY AND ENGLISH BENCHMARKS READING: EARLY LEVEL

### ENJOYMENT AND CHOICE

I enjoy exploring and playing with the patterns and sounds of language and can use what I learn.
LIT 0-01a / LIT 0-11a / LIT 0-20a

I enjoy exploring and choosing stories and other texts to watch, read or listen to, and can share my likes and dislikes.
LIT 0-01b / LIT 0-11b

• Chooses a story or other texts for enjoyment making use of the cover, title, author and/or illustrator.

• Engages with and enjoys watching, reading or listening to different texts, including stories, songs and rhymes, and can share likes and dislikes.

### TOOLS FOR READING

I explore sounds, letters and words, discovering how they work together, and I can use what I learn to help me as I read and write.
ENG 0-12a / LIT 0-13a / LIT 0-21a

• Hears and says patterns in words.
• Hears and says the different single sounds made by letters.
• Hears and says blends/sounds made by a combination of letters.
• Knows the difference between a letter, word and numeral.
• Reads from left to right and top to bottom.
• Uses knowledge of sounds, letters and patterns to read words.
• Uses knowledge of sight vocabulary/tricky words to read familiar words in context.
• Reads aloud familiar texts with attention to simple punctuation.
• Uses context clues to support understanding of different texts.

### FINDING AND USING INFORMATION

I use signs, books or other texts to find useful or interesting information and I use this to plan, make choices or learn new things.
LIT 0-14a

• Finds information in a text to learn new things.
• Shows an awareness of a few features of fiction and non-fiction texts when using/choosing texts for particular purposes.

### UNDERSTANDING, ANALYSING, EVALUATING

To help me understand stories and other texts, I ask questions and link what I am learning with what I already know.
LIT 0-07a / LIT 0-16a / ENG 0-17a

I enjoy exploring events and characters in stories and other texts, sharing my thoughts in different ways.
LIT 0-19a

• Engages with texts read to them.
• Asks and answers questions about events and ideas in a text.
• Answers questions to help predict what will happen next.
• Contributes to discussions about events, characters and ideas relevant to the text.
• Shares thoughts and feelings about stories and other texts in different ways.
• Retells familiar stories in different ways, for example, role play, puppets and/or drawings.
• Relates information and ideas from a text to personal experiences.

# LITERACY AND ENGLISH BENCHMARKS READING: FIRST LEVEL

## ENJOYMENT AND CHOICE

I regularly select and read, listen to or watch texts which I enjoy and find interesting, and I can explain why I prefer certain texts and authors.
LIT 1-11a / LIT 2-11a

- Selects different texts regularly for enjoyment or for a specific purpose using, for example, cover, title, author, illustrator and/or blurb.

- Explains preferences for particular texts and authors.

## TOOLS FOR READING

I can use my knowledge of sight vocabulary, phonics, context clues, punctuation and grammar to read with understanding and expression.
ENG 1-12a

I am learning to select and use strategies and resources before I read, and as I read, to help make the meaning of texts clear.
LIT 1-13a

- Reads aloud a familiar piece of text adding expression and can show understanding.
- Reads an increasing number of common/high frequency words, key reading words, core topic words and words of personal significance.
- Uses a range of word recognition strategies independently.
- Decodes unknown words by locating and pronouncing familiar letter patterns and blends.
- Uses context clues to read and understand texts.
- Uses punctuation and grammar to read with understanding and expression.

## FINDING AND USING INFORMATION

Using what I know about the features of different types of texts, I can find, select, sort and use information for a specific purpose.
LIT 1-14a

I am learning to make notes under given headings and use them to understand information, explore ideas and problems and create new texts.
LIT 1-15a

- Identifies and finds key information in fiction and non-fiction texts using content page, index, headings, sub-headings and diagrams to help locate information.

- Makes notes under given headings for different purposes.

## UNDERSTANDING, ANALYSING, EVALUATING

To show my understanding across different areas of learning, I can identify and consider the purpose and main ideas of a text.
LIT 1-16a

To show my understanding, I can respond to different kinds of questions and other close reading tasks and I am learning to create some questions of my own.
ENG 1-17a

To help me develop an informed view, I can recognise the difference between fact and opinion.
LIT 1-18a

I can share my thoughts about structure, characters and/or setting, recognise the writer's message and relate it to my own experiences, and comment on the effective choice of words and other features.

ENG 1-19a

- Identifies the main ideas of texts.

- Makes appropriate suggestions about the purpose of a text.

- Answers literal, inferential and evaluative questions about texts.

- Asks questions to help make sense of a text.

- Recognises the difference between fact and opinion.

- Offers own ideas about characters, writer's use of language, structure and/or setting.

- Offers own ideas about the writer's message and, when appropriate, relates these to personal experiences.

# LITERACY AND ENGLISH BENCHMARKS READING: SECOND LEVEL

## ENJOYMENT AND CHOICE

I regularly select and read, listen to or watch texts which I enjoy and find interesting, and I can explain why I prefer certain texts and authors.
LIT 1-11a / LIT 2-11a

• Selects texts regularly for enjoyment or to find information for a specific purpose.
• Explains preferences for particular texts, authors or sources with supporting detail.

## TOOLS FOR READING

Through developing my knowledge of context clues, punctuation, grammar and layout, I can read unfamiliar texts with increasing fluency, understanding and expression.
ENG 2-12a / ENG 3-12a / ENG 4-12a

I can select and use a range of strategies and resources before I read, and as I read, to make meaning clear and give reasons for my selection.
LIT 2-13a

• Reads with fluency, understanding and expression using appropriate pace and tone.

• Uses knowledge of context clues, punctuation, grammar and layout to read unfamiliar texts with understanding.

• Applies a range of reading skills and strategies to read and understand texts, for example, skimming, scanning, predicting, clarifying and/or summarising.

## FINDING AND USING INFORMATION

Using what I know about the features of different types of texts, I can find, select and sort information from a variety of sources and use this for different purposes.
LIT 2-14a

I can make notes, organise them under suitable headings and use them to understand information, develop my thinking, explore problems and create new texts, using my own words as appropriate.
LIT 2-15a

• Skims texts to identify purpose and main ideas.
• Scans texts to find key information.

• Finds, selects and sorts relevant information from a range of sources.

• Makes and organises notes using own words, for the most part.
• Uses notes to create new texts that show understanding of the topic or issue.

## UNDERSTANDING, ANALYSING, EVALUATING

To show my understanding across different areas of learning, I can identify and consider the purpose and main ideas of a text and use supporting detail.
LIT 2-16a

To show my understanding, I can respond to literal, inferential and evaluative questions and other close reading tasks and can create different kinds of questions of my own.
ENG 2-17a

To help me develop an informed view, I can identify and explain the difference between fact and opinion, recognise when I am being influenced, and have assessed how useful and believable my sources are.
LIT 2-18a

I can:
• discuss structure, characterisation and/or setting;
• recognise the relevance of the writer's theme and how this relates to my own and others' experiences; and
• discuss the writer's style and other features appropriate to genre.
ENG 2-19a

• Identifies the purpose of a text with suitable explanation.
• Identifies the main ideas of a text with appropriate detail.
• Makes relevant comments about features of language, for example, vocabulary, sentence structure and punctuation.
• Responds to a range of questions, including literal, inferential and evaluative questions, to demonstrate understanding of texts.
• Creates different types of questions to show understanding of texts.
• Distinguishes between fact and opinion with appropriate explanation.
• Recognises techniques used to influence the reader, for example, word choice, emotive language, rhetorical questions and/or repetition.
• Identifies which sources are most useful/reliable.
• Makes relevant comments about structure, characterisation and/or setting with reference to the text.
• Relates the writer's theme to own and/or others' experiences.
• Makes relevant comments about aspects of the writer's style, use of language and other features appropriate to genre, with reference to the text.

# LITERACY AND ENGLISH BENCHMARKS READING: THIRD LEVEL

## ENJOYMENT AND CHOICE

I regularly select and read, listen to or watch texts for enjoyment and interest, and I can express how well they meet my needs and expectations and give reasons, with evidence, for my personal response. I can identify sources to develop the range of my reading.
LIT 3-11a

• Selects texts regularly for enjoyment and interest or relevant sources to inform thinking.
• Gives a personal response to texts with appropriate justification.
• Explains how well a text or source meets needs and expectations with appropriate justification.

## TOOLS FOR READING

Through developing my knowledge of context clues, punctuation, grammar and layout, I can read unfamiliar texts with increasing fluency, understanding and expression.
ENG 2-12a / ENG 3-12a / ENG 4-12a

I can select and use the strategies and resources I find most useful before I read, and as I read, to monitor and check my understanding.
LIT 3-13a

• Reads texts with fluency, understanding and expression using appropriate pace and tone.

• Applies knowledge of context clues, word roots, grammar, punctuation, sentence and text structures to read unfamiliar texts with understanding.

• Applies a range of strategies to engage with and interrogate texts, for example, skimming, scanning, predicting, clarifying, summarising and analysing.

## FINDING AND USING INFORMATION

Using what I know about the features of different types of texts, I can find, select, sort, summarise, link and use information from different sources.
LIT 3-14a / LIT 4-14a

I can make notes and organise them to develop my thinking, help retain and recall information, explore issues and create new texts, using my own words as appropriate.
LIT 3-15a / LIT 4-15a

• Finds, selects and sorts relevant information from a variety of sources for a range of purposes.

• Summarises key information using own words.

• Uses own words to make and organise notes, selecting key information and linking ideas from more than one source.

• Uses notes to create new texts that show understanding of the topic or issue and draw on information from more than one source.

## UNDERSTANDING, ANALYSING, EVALUATING

To show my understanding across different areas of learning, I can:
• identify and consider the purpose, main concerns or concepts and use supporting detail;
• make inferences from key statements;
• identify and discuss similarities and differences between different types of text.
LIT 3-16a

To show my understanding, I can comment, with evidence, on the content and form of short and extended texts, and respond to literal, inferential and evaluative questions and other types of close reading tasks.
ENG 3-17a

To help me develop an informed view, I am exploring the techniques used to influence my opinion. I can recognise persuasion and assess the reliability of information and credibility and value of my sources.
LIT 3-18a

I can: • discuss and evaluate the structure, characterisation and/or setting using some supporting evidence;
• identify the main theme of the text and recognise the relevance this has to my own and others' experiences; and
• identify and comment on aspects of the writer's style and other features appropriate to genre using some relevant evidence.
ENG 3-19a

• Identifies purpose and audience of a range of texts with appropriate justification.
• Gives an accurate account of the main ideas of texts.
• Makes inferences and deductions with appropriate justification.
• Identifies similarities and differences between texts and makes appropriate comments about content, style and/or language.
• Responds to a range of close reading questions, including literal, inferential and evaluative questions, to show understanding of texts and knowledge of language.
• Identifies features of language and gives an appropriate explanation of the effect they have on the reader, for example, word choice, sentence structure, punctuation, grammar and/or imagery.
• Identifies and makes appropriate comments about persuasive language such as word choice, emotive language, repetition, rhetorical questions and/or use of statistics.
• Comments on reliability and relevance/usefulness of sources with appropriate justification.
• Makes evaluative comments about structure, characterisation and/or setting with relevant reference to the text.
• Shows understanding of the writer's theme and can link it to own or others' experiences.
• Identifies and makes evaluative comments about aspects of the writer's style, use of language and other features appropriate to genre with supporting evidence.

# LITERACY AND ENGLISH BENCHMARKS READING: FOURTH LEVEL

## ENJOYMENT AND CHOICE

I regularly select and read texts for enjoyment and interest, and I can express how well they meet my needs and expectations and give reasons, with evidence, for my personal response.
I can independently identify sources to develop the range of my reading.
LIT 4-11a

• Selects regularly and independently, texts for enjoyment and interest or relevant sources to inform thinking.
• Gives a personal response to spoken texts or explains how well a spoken text or source meets needs and expectations, justifying opinion with relevant reference to the text.

## TOOLS FOR READING

Through developing my knowledge of context clues, punctuation, grammar and layout, I can read unfamiliar texts with increasing fluency, understanding and expression.
ENG 2-12a / ENG 3-12a / ENG 4-12a

Before and as I read, I can apply strategies and use resources independently to help me read a wide variety of texts and/or find the information I need.
LIT 4-13a

• Reads with fluency, understanding and expression across a wide range of texts.

• Applies knowledge of language such as word roots, grammar, punctuation, tone, sentence and text structures to read texts with understanding.
• Applies a range of strategies to engage with and interrogate texts, for example, skimming, scanning, predicting, clarifying, summarising, analysing and annotating.

## FINDING AND USING INFORMATION

Using what I know about the features of different types of texts, I can find, select, sort, summarise, link and use information from different sources.
LIT 3-14a / LIT 4-14a

I can make notes and organise them to develop my thinking, help retain and recall information, explore issues and create new texts, using my own words as appropriate.
LIT 3-15a / LIT 4-15a

• Finds, selects and sorts essential information from a variety of sources for a range of purposes.
• Summarises key information, from more than one source, using own words.

• Uses own words to make and organise notes, synthesising key information from different sources.
• Uses notes to create new texts that show an understanding of the topic or issue, synthesising information from different sources.

## UNDERSTANDING, ANALYSING, EVALUATING

Using what I know about the features of different types of texts, I can find, select, sort, summarise, link and use information from different sources.
LIT 3-14a / LIT 4-14a

I can make notes and organise them to develop my thinking, help retain and recall information, explore issues and create new texts, using my own words as appropriate.
LIT 3-15a / LIT 4-15a

To show my understanding across different areas of learning, I can: • clearly state the purpose, main concerns, concepts or arguments and use supporting detail; •make inferences from key statements and state these accurately in my own words; and • compare and contrast different types of text.
LIT 4-16a

To show my understanding, I can give detailed, evaluative comments, with evidence, on the content and form of short and extended texts, and respond to different kinds of questions and other types of close reading tasks.
ENG 4-17a

To help me develop an informed view, I can recognise persuasion and bias, identify some of the techniques used to influence my opinion, and assess the reliability of information and credibility and value of my sources.
LIT 4-18a

I can:

• discuss and evaluate the effectiveness of structure, characterisation and/or setting using some supporting evidence; • identify how the writer's main theme or central concerns are revealed and can recognise how they relate to my own and others' experiences; and
• identify and make a personal evaluation of the effect of aspects of the writer's style and other features appropriate to genre using some relevant evidence and terminology.
ENG 4-19a

• States clearly the purpose, audience and main ideas of a range of texts with appropriate justification.
• Makes accurate inferences with appropriate justification.
• Compares and contrasts the content, style and language of different texts with supporting detail.
• Responds in detail to a range of close reading questions to show understanding of texts and knowledge and understanding of language.
• Makes evaluative comments about the effect of features of language, for example, word choice, sentence structure, punctuation, grammar and/or imagery.
• Identifies the use of bias and persuasion and comments appropriately on some of the techniques used, for example, word choice, emotive language, repetition, rhetorical questions, use of statistics and/or hyperbole.
• Makes evaluative comments about relevance, reliability and credibility of sources, with appropriate justification.
• Makes evaluative comments about the effectiveness of structure, characterisation and/or setting with relevant reference to the text.
• Shows understanding of how the writer's theme is developed and recognises how it relates to own or others' experiences/the writer's purpose/the central concerns of the text.
• Identifies and makes evaluative comments on aspects of the writer's style, use of language and other features appropriate to genre with detailed reference to the text and appropriate terminology.

### 'SUCK IT AND SEE'

As with all of the resources in this book, they are provided on a 'suck it and see' basis. That is, you need to try them and see how they work for you and your class. You should feel that the resources are a valuable addition to what you're doing and that you can feel or see the benefits e.g. you feel more focussed with your planning for reading, for groups and the class as a whole; children are more confident talking about their reading progress and preferences. Tweak or adapt to suit your own practice.

A P6/Y5 teacher in one of the *Reflective Reading* pilot schools decided to use the *Child Friendly Assessment Booklets* at the end of every week, rather than termly. She explained that they kept the booklets in the front of the children's Language jotters and it was easy to discuss progress and what they'd been learning at the end of the week, while it was still fresh in everyone's mind. And that's great— your classroom time is limited make sure that whatever 'new' thing is being introduced that there is a tangible 'return on investment'—that it's worth it.

### THE ASSESSMENT GIRAFFE

Why is there a giraffe on the *Child Friendly Assessment Booklets* and what does a giraffe have to do with assessment? Well, Jeffrey the giraffe, as well as being extremely intelligent, handsome, and good at telling jokes, actually performs an important function in the classroom: he encourages formative assessment, reminding children to reflect on their reading and learning, and reminding teachers to do a plenary and 'join the dots' of the learning that's taken place.

Jeffrey is always asking questions such as: *How are you doing? What did you learn today? What do you find difficult today? What did you like best this week? How have you improved since last time? What will you do differently next time? What can you do now, that you couldn't do on Monday?* And so on… In this way, children will begin to be able to talk confidently about their strengths and successes as well as identifying their own 'next steps'.

### PLENARY PUPPETS*

One particularly effective way is to use a 'plenary puppet'—a giraffe preferably— but of course any animal or character would do. Children will be desperate to tell Jeffrey, or whoever, exactly what they've been learning and how they've been progressing. This is a great habit to develop, especially at the end of the week or the end of a block of work, or the end of a book. In the buzz of a busy classroom when you're always working against the clock, the truth is that the plenary is the thing that we tend to miss out—or allow to drop off the end of the lesson. (Unless you're being observed of course!)

*Not partial to puppets? Masks can work as well. Which VIP will 'visit' to find out about your learning? The Queen? Simon Cowell or how about Dug the Plenary Pug?

Adding a simple assessment display to your classroom can act as a 'visual hook' that reminds all of us to reflect on our learning. You could have a picture of your puppet, VIP or pug on the wall; add laminated speech bubbles with plenary questions to use at the end of a lesson, the end of the day, or the end of the week.

## TEACHER JUDGEMENT: AN INFORMED OVERVIEW

While the resources in this chapter are tools for planning and assessing reading, we must never forget that every day we have lots of information at our fingertips about how our children are getting on with reading. It is important to consider the 'bigger picture' including children's daily experiences, as well as statements and benchmarks. To build up a complete and valid assessment picture, the documents in this chapter should be used along side and in addition to:

- **day-to-day classroom observations**
- **discussions and learning conversations**
- **written work including what children *Say, Make, Do* and *Write***
- **assessments and tests**

What did you learn today?

say make do write

### THE PHONICS SCREENING CHECK: AN ASSESSMENT WORTH ADOPTING

Introduced in England in 2012, before systematic synthetic phonics was mandated as the sole method of reading instruction, The Phonics Screening Check is a valuable, light-touch assessment and only takes around 6 minutes per child to administer.

I would urge all schools, especially those in Scotland, to adopt the check; currently it is being trialled in Australia. Not only is it a useful tool to check alphabetic code knowledge and blending skill, as it uses both real words and nonsense words, but it also provides robust, trackable data. Most importantly however, it identifies children who are struggling and/ or at risk of reading failure.

It is freely available online (search for 'phonics screening check' to download test papers and instructions) and can be used as a diagnostic assessment at any time, or as a summative assessment at the end of P2/Y1, by which time 100% of children should be passing the check with ease.

**SCORES ON THE DOORS**

Percentage of children in England who reached the expected standard:

2012: 58%
2013: 69%
2014: 74%
2015: 77%
2016: 81%

How would your class do…?

CHAPTER 4

# Teaching and Learning: Short Read

# CHAPTER 4
# Teaching & Learning: Short Read

## YOUR READING WEEK

*Reflective Reading* has been designed to cover all reading needs and can be used Monday to Thursday, leaving Friday free for extended writing.

Reading should take place on at least four days out of five. The table below gives a suggested overview of how your week could be structured. (Days are of course flexible e.g. a teacher may prefer to do *Short Read* on a Thursday for example, this is fine.)

In this chapter we will explore *Short Read* in detail, and then *Long Read* will be covered in Chapter 5.

## WHAT IS SHORT READ?

*Short Read* takes place once a week (I used to do it on a Monday) and is a whole-class comprehension lesson. During the lesson children work in mixed ability trios to read and answer questions on a short text* or extract from a longer text.

*Remember that for text choice, anything goes; be mindful of the 'Definition of Text' on page 4. A *Short Read* lesson could be based on any of the following texts—but it must be able to be comfortably addressed and fully explored within one, stand-alone lesson.

| Reflective Reading Weekly Overview | | |
|---|---|---|
| Monday | Tues, Weds, Thurs | Friday |
| **Short Read** | **Long Read** | **Extended Writing** |
| Weekly session covering wide variety of texts* and extracts. (Whole-class; mixed ability groups) | Daily sessions using novels, reading books or a 'main text*' on consecutive days. Arranged by ability groups; opportunities for whole-class teaching as required. | Writing lesson and extended writing session. (For best results writing topic may link to reading) |
| **Reading for pleasure and learning everyday** | | |

- **picture books (especially in early years/lower stages—but also at every stage)**
- **film clips, adverts, trailers and short films, an episode from a series**
- **poems, short stories, fiction extracts**
- **non-fiction articles, reports and extracts**
- **real texts such as recipes, leaflets, flyers, packaging etc.**

I highly recommend using *Short Read* as an ideal opportunity to put non-fiction texts back on the menu. Often schools have timetables in place that prioritise fiction, without realising it. Reading books and novels used in class for the purposes of teaching reading usually focus on fiction. Occasionally, teachers might use non-fiction texts as part of project or topic work, but I always ask, is that a topic lesson or is it a reading lesson?

## TO USE OR NOT TO USE TEXTBOOKS?

The textbooks that used to be used for comprehension in the classroom, which by their nature provided a variety of texts, have all but disappeared from the educational landscape in primary schools in Scotland since the introduction of *Curriculum for Excellence,* along with an unfortunate and misguided belief that 'textbooks are bad'. Many 'schemes' ended up in the bin, but they were never replaced with something better.

To be clear, I believe textbooks do have a place; teachers should have all of the resources they need at their fingertips and should be able to pick and choose the right tool for the job in hand (without having to constantly create their own resources). However, I also recognise

that, when it comes to non-fiction, the schemes that were dumped were long past their sell-by-date. When you're reading about Mother Teresa as if she's still alive or about America during President Clinton's stint, then *'Houston, we have a problem.'*

Non-fiction dates quickly. When schools buy textbooks you can often be stuck with them for 20 years... or longer. The easiest and cheapest way to find something that's relevant and up to date is to print something off the internet. The good thing about doing this, is that you'll be effectively 'killing two birds with one stone'. You'll be doing a reading lesson, but improving children's general knowledge at the same time—which is what is so crucial for comprehension. Also, as you will be choosing the text, you will be able to ensure that it's **relevant**. By relevant, I mean that it links to a novel you're reading, a topic you're studying in science or in RME (religious and moral education), a project you're doing such as the Victorians—or it might be something that catches your eye in the news. *Did someone just say Dr Who is going to be a \*woman\*?*

## MIXED ABILITY TRIOS

*Why* are children working in mixed ability trios? This is the first thing that usually strikes teachers as being unusual, because, well, normally when we do a reading lesson, we group by ability. You know, we'll have our groups, that are named something like the *Eagles*, the *Buzzards*, the *Sparrows* —and the *Worms*. Ok. I know you're not that cruel, but you know exactly what I mean. Worse still, so do our children.

What I can tell you is this. Put a child in

the Worms (or the Triangles, or the Yellow group) in Primary 1 (YR) and they are pretty much guaranteed to still be in the equivalent group in Primary 7 (Y6) having successfully fulfilled the low expectations we projected onto them for their entire school career.

I know this comes from a good place. I know we believe we are doing what's right for each child at the time. But perhaps we should consider, for a moment, that differentiation in this way is part of the problem—and we just keep shifting the problem onto the teacher in the next class, and so on, until at some point you're trying to juggle six reading groups, two individuals and a 'spread of ability' that is impossible to manage.

## "Available evidence shows that involving children working with each other in small groups helps to close the attainment gap."
### SOSU & ELLIS
### CLOSING THE ATTAINMENT GAP IN SCOTTISH EDUCATION

By creating groups we are actually growing gaps, rather than closing them—particularly when it comes to basic skills that everyone needs. Controversial? Yes and no. Try to find research that supports setting and streaming... you'll struggle. Recent research actually shows that working in small, mixed ability groups is beneficial for children from disadvantaged households and helps to close the attainment gap. (Joseph Rowntree Report,

Sosu & Ellis, *Closing the attainment gap in Scottish education* )

In a *Short Read* lesson, by working in mixed ability trios, we are attempting to re-engage the reluctant readers; re-motivate them by showing them that reading lessons can be fun and rewarding. Within the trio, you can assign roles:

**Reader:** reads the text to the group if required
**Recorder:** writes down any answers
**Manager:** keeps everything organised and monitors time

Use stickers, lanyards, badges to indicate each person's job. To be honest, the job that really matters the most is the *Reader* because they are going to be the ones to read the text aloud, to ensure everyone can access it. When you are creating your trios, make sure that you allocate the role of reader to someone who can actually read.

Does it have to be a trio? No. See what works for you, but in my experience, four is too many to get round a text comfortably and it allows people to stay in the background, and with pairs you invariably end up with the Reader doing all of the work, while the other person mentally 'checks out'.

## WHOLE-CLASS TEACHING

During the trio activities, much of the work is carried out through listening, talking and discussion; writing is limited to recording answers to ensure everyone feels they are participating fully. Team work and a group effort is emphasised— there is also a competitive element as the trios try to 'win' and get the most points/ best answers.

The other really big pay-off is that because children are in mixed ability groups—suddenly this is a whole-class lesson about reading—where, whenever you want to, you can actually teach everyone at the same time, which is a luxury. (Do not be afraid of teaching your class. If you want them to learn things then it's your job to teach them. Ignore pressure to avoid 'chalk & talk'; direct teaching works and is supported by research.) Provide explicit instruction, model and demonstrate how to find answers; there will be teaching points aplenty if you choose your text wisely.

Another big advantage is that by changing text types every Monday (or whenever) you will actually cover an impressive range of text types across the term/session and provide **breadth** of reading.

I've highlighted **relevance** and **breadth** in this section as they are actually two of the *Seven Principles* of *Curriculum for Excellence*. Any lesson, or series of lessons, should be designed with these in mind. No matter what country you're in, or what curriculum you're following, I think these principles are worth bearing in mind. They are, I think, my favourite part of *Curriculum for Excellence*, but teachers tend to forget about them. On the next page I'd like you to meet, then: *The Chickens for Excellence.*

## CHOOSING TEXTS: WHAT MAKES A TEXT 'RELEVANT'?

Relevant texts for Short Read lessons might include texts that:

- link to other curricular areas being studied
- are relevant because they are topical, current or in the news (local, national or international)
- link to other books/texts being read e.g texts that offer another viewpoint, enhance our understanding of a theme or subject
- are culturally relevant/important e.g. Burns, Shakespeare, Anne Frank's Diary
- are relevant to everyday life e.g. timetables, advertising, election materials

For example, if we're reading Charlie and the Chocolate Factory as our class novel, I might choose Short Read texts based around the following themes that add to our knowledge, provide a good example of a text type e.g. functional writing, or illustrate elements of the 'Writer's Craft' that we want to study and so on:
redundancy and employment, manners today, the Seven Deadly Sins, healthy eating, obesity, Roald Dahl's life and work, Roald Dahl's 'Television' poem, how chocolate is made, a chocolate recipe, sweets and dental health, children's hobbies today, Dahl's character descriptions etc. etc.

If Roald Dahl was writing today, would there still be a character called Mike Teavee—or would he be called Mike Gamer, Mike Alltech or Mike. U. Tube?

Challenge and Enjoyment

1st?
1st?

Depth

Breadth

Personalisation and Choice

Progression

Coherence

Relevance

Chickens for Excellence

## CHICKENS FOR EXCELLENCE

Let's consider how the *Seven Principles* of *Curriculum for Excellence* apply to reading.

*Challenge and enjoyment.* I love that our curriculum includes the word 'enjoyment' in it. I don't think it's too much to ask for children to enjoy learning most of the time at school, particularly in primary. *Challenge* speaks for itself. Sometimes, 'pitching' the text at the right level, especially if it's a whole-class reading activity, can be tricky. But there does need to be a certain level of challenge, or what's the point? What I have found with the *Short Read* lessons is that, because of the high levels of motivation to read the text and complete the 'quiz', texts can often be more challenging than you would normally expect.

*Depth.* Reading texts deeply, considering their themes, their messages and the questions they raise is important. Also, reading full texts, rather than extracts, reading the full novel, watching the full film, allows us to explore and evaluate the text in its entirety.

*Breadth.* Breadth of reading and reading lots of different text types is crucial. One OECD study showed that children who read a wider variety of texts are better readers—it's common sense really. Through *Short Read*, children will build up a familiarity with lots of text types, and this will also help when they come to writing.

*Personalisation and choice.* We all like choices, they empower us and give us a voice. Children of course will get to choose their ERIC time books, but it's also worth allowing choice (when practical and possible) when choosing novels or texts for study. I would recommend building up to this level of choice though e.g. I sometimes let P7 (Y6) choose a novel for individual study for the last few weeks of term. When we cover *Long Read* in the next chapter we will also build choice into our tasks.

*Progression.* Well, that's what we need to see; whether it's progression in the mechanics of reading, motivation, or comprehension, or whether it's more sophisticated texts, responses and discussions—there has to be progress— it's what we go to school for!

*Coherence.* Your literacy curriculum has to make sense; fit together sensibly with other areas of the curriculum and be well organised to ensure coverage and progression over the term and year.

*Relevance.* We've mentioned this already, but it's important. You have to be able to answer the questions: *Why are we reading this? What does it have to do with anything? Why are we reading* **this**, *rather than* **that**? Reading choices need to be relevant in some way, and you should be prepared to justify them and explain why ***they're worth it***.

*OK,* enough background and rationale— let's get on with telling you about some of the activities you'll be doing as part of your *Short Read* lesson...

## INTRODUCING 'TEXTPLORERS'

**T**exTplorers are close reading activities designed to be used with short texts or extracts from longer texts. They are ideal to use during *Short Read* sessions once a week.

TexTplorers isn't new; I've just renamed a collection of strategies that were developed by Eric Lunzer and Keith Gardner* at Nottingham University in the late 70s, which they then expanded on in their book *Learning from the Written Word* in 1984. They called their strategies DARTS —which stands for *Directed Activities Related to Texts*.

DARTs were originally created for use in the secondary classroom, but I came across them when I was teaching in East Ayrshire and my class loved them. I don't think they really got the recognition in Scotland that they deserve; they work at both primary and secondary level, and I'm convinced we should be using them more often. Perhaps one of the reasons DARTs never dominated in Scotland was because of some of the strategies and their names. For example, one of the first exercises I tried with my P5 (Y4) was a *'Selective Substitution'*—now *I* had no clue what that meant—never mind the children in my class...

I've chosen seven DARTs that I feel lend themselves to use in the primary classroom and I've renamed those too— so that they now do *'what it says on the tin'.*

*In case you're hearing warning bells or you're wondering if this is the same 'Gardner' that had the 'theory of multiple intelligences' you can relax, it's not him— that was Howard Gardner.

## THE TEXTPLORER ADVANTAGE

- TexTplorers are good because they have a game-like quality; their quiz-like nature means that everyone is involved, engaged and learning—but it doesn't feel like work.
- They allow children to get 'up close & personal' with texts; they have to read the text very closely to be able to find the answers.
- Through discussion and modelling, TexTplorers make the reading process explicit; less able learners benefit from this high quality discussion and thinking.
- In a group, the text can be more challenging as there is a high level of motivation within the trios. (I once used a text straight from the normal Wikipedia with a P3-P5/Y2-Y4 class without amendment. It was a challenging text, but as it was about Moshi Monsters, they were all keen to read and find the answers.)

## YOU WILL NEED

- Mixed ability trios with stickers, badges or lanyards printed with roles of 'Reader', 'Recorder' and 'Manager'
- Chopsticks or wooden lollipop sticks with googly eye for 'Follow the Reader' (one each)
- Timer (on whiteboard or sand timer)
- Highlighters or coloured pencils for text marking
- High quality, high interest text* or extract*

## WARM-UP TASKS

**B**efore diving into the TexTplorers main activity I often do one or more of the following warm-up tasks:

# TexTplorers

## RECONSTRUCTION ACTIVITIES USING ADAPTED TEXTS

**BLANKETY BLANK:** (or 'cloze procedure') remove words to create 'blanks' to be filled in. Choose a mixture of words to eliminate, or try blanking out only nouns, verbs, adverbs or adjectives. (Scoring: 2 points for the correct word, 1 point for additional words that fit the context and make sense)

**JIGSAW JUMBLE:** single words, sentences, paragraphs or pictures to be rearranged into proper sequence. Can be used as a quick warm-up.

**SPOT THE SILLY WORD:** insert inappropriate or 'silly words' that will be spotted through close reading e.g. polar bears mainly eat crisps. Children must spot the erroneous words and suggest the correct or 'sensible' word.

**PREDICT WHAT HAPPENS NEXT:** incomplete text given so children must discuss and decide what they think happens next. Use chronological order, or give the beginning and end of text so children need to discuss and predict what's missing from 'the middle'.

## ANALYSIS ACTIVITIES USING TEXTS 'AS IS'

**PICTURE IT:** using description from the text, children must draw a scene, character, map or object. Highlighting text is useful here. May include quotes from text around drawing.

**TEXT MARKING:** highlight, underline or label, key words, VCOP, facts and opinions, arguments for and against, character descriptions/evidence etc.

**INTEGRATE IT:** use the text to complete diagrams, visual tables, flowcharts, timelines, timetables and present information gleaned from text. Particularly good for non-fiction texts.

TexTplorers
COMPREHENSION
IN THE CAN*
*may contain teaching

## NAME THAT TEXT

Remember the TV programme *Name that Tune*? It's like that, except you give the class ten seconds to identify the text type using the structure, layout and visual clues. *I'll name that text in ten...* Most children when asked will have a stab at the text type: It's a news article/diary/novel—which is great, but always ask: how do they know? What gave the game away? Was it the column layout, the first person narrative, the title, the subheadings—or something else?

## JUST THE GIST

Before reading properly, instruct the class to do a quick skim read to identify the subject matter and what the text is about e.g. what are we going to be reading about today? Set a short timer around 20-30 seconds. Allow thinking time and group answer.

## FOLLOW THE READER

This is when the *Reader* in the trio will read the text aloud to the group. We want to be sure however, that everyone is paying attention to the text as it's being read, rather than staring out of the window. To solve this, I give each group member a wooden chopstick; they use this to follow underneath the words as they are read aloud. (If you're worried about certain class members having pointy wooden sticks, simply use lollipop sticks instead with a googly eye stuck on the end. One school I know call these their 'I-Readers'. ) The sticks are supposed to provide focus and a be a little bit of fun. I tell any class that if they can't handle the fun, all the wee 'gimmicks' will be taken away. (Another thing that chopsticks can be used for is silent reading. Speed readers actually use a reading stick to help their eye glide across the page. That's what I started out using the chopsticks for originally.)

## WHAT SHOULD TEXTPLORERS LOOK LIKE?

If someone walks into your room during the group part of the lesson then the impression should be one of fun and high engagement and purposefulness, with an emphasis on group work and talking and listening.

However, it will all be a bit pointless if you don't take time to tease out the learning and high quality discussion. It's key to encourage children to explain the thinking behind their answers, referring to the text and any clues or evidence that they used. Asking questions like 'Why?' and 'How do you know?' will help reveal their reasoning. Take as many opportunities as you wish to explore teaching points that might crop up.

Over the next few pages I'm going to provide you with some sample TexTplorers activities, which hopefully you'll be able to try out in class almost straight away. Before jumping into any of these activities in class, you will already have completed a warm-up and your trios will have already read the text together.

When I'm modelling lessons, I also tend to have a short starter (and a finisher when time allows) of some kind, which might be a game, a poem, some 'Textercises' to music—so that everyone is upbeat and ready to listen. Recently, I did five minutes of meditation using an app with a Primary 3 (Y2) class as we were going to be focussing on listening for our *Reflective Reading* lesson—it worked a treat!

## ORGANISATION & RESOURCES

- Mixed ability trios with stickers, badges or lanyards printed with roles of 'Reader', 'Recorder' and 'Manager'
- Chopsticks or lollipop sticks for Follow the Reader (one per child)
- Timer (on whiteboard or sand timer)
- Highlighters or coloured pencils for text marking
- High quality, high interest text* or extract

## TOP TIPS

- TexTplorers should be fun and engaging with the emphasis on group work, discussion and talking and listening.
- Encourage children to explain the thinking behind their answers referring to the text and any clues or evidence that they used.
- Asking questions like 'Why?' and 'How do you know?' will help reveal their reasoning.

## WARM-UP BEFORE READING

**Name that Text:** I'll name that text in ten seconds... Identify the text type using structure, layout and visual clues.

**Just the Gist:** a skim reading exercise to identify subject/contents, what the text is about, can be timed. Allow thinking time and group answer.

**Follow the Reader:** 'Reader' in group takes the lead and reads text aloud while other group members listen and follow the text with their chopsticks, or 'Magic Reading Sticks'.

## RECONSTRUCTION ACTIVITIES USING ADAPTED TEXTS

**Blankety Blank** (or 'cloze procedure') remove words to create 'blanks' to be filled in. Choose a mixture of words to eliminate, or try blanking out only nouns, verbs, adverbs or adjectives. (2 points for the correct word, 1 point for additional words that fit the context and make sense)

**Jigsaw Jumble** single words, sentences, paragraphs or pictures to be rearranged into proper sequence. Can be used as a quick warm-up.

**Spot the Silly Word** insert inappropriate or 'silly words' that will be spotted through close reading e.g. polar bears mainly eat crisps. Children must spot the erroneous words and suggest the correct or 'sensible' word.

**Predict What Happens Next** incomplete text given so children must discuss and decide what they think happens next. Use chronological order, or give the beginning and end of text so children need to discuss and predict what's missing from 'the middle'.

## ANALYSIS ACTIVITIES USING TEXTS 'AS IS'

**Picture It** using description from the text, children must draw a scene, character, map or object. Highlighting text useful. May include quotes from text around drawing as evidence.

**Text Marking** highlight, underline or label, key words, main points, VCOP, facts and opinions, arguments for and against, writer's craft tools (simile, metaphor etc.) unknown words etc.

**Integrate It** use the text to complete diagrams, visual tables, flowcharts, timelines, timetables and present information gleaned from text. Particularly good for non-fiction texts.

## TEXTPLORERS ACTIVITIES

### BLANKETY BLANK

**W**ell, there's no prizes for guessing that this is going to be a cloze procedure activity! Trios simply have to work out what word should go in the empty space; there will be points for correct answers. What do points make? PRIZES! I always give a small prize (sticker, special chopsticks, rubber, pencil or bookmark etc.) to the winning trio for this one—it helps to heighten the competitive spirit, but also the feeling of team work and effort.

What is different in this cloze procedure though is that there isn't only one right answer, you're allowed lots of right answers—as long as they 'fit' and make sense within the context. This is where the teamwork and discussion come in.

For scoring, you can make up your own rules, but here's what I do:

- **2 points for every correct\* answer (\*the word the author _actually_ used)**

- **1 extra point for every other answer, that they come up with in their group, that fits and makes sense with the context.**

I always emphasise that the winning trio will be the one that works together to find as many extra answers and points as possible.

For example:

**_Mary pushed the coin through the _____ in the porcelain pig's back._**

The 'real' answer—the one that the author

used is **_'slot'_** in this case. Groups will also get an extra point for any/all of the following words (and any other ones that fit that I haven't thought of):

**_slit, gap, hole, opening, space, crack_**

You can award extra points at your discretion. If a group was to offer a particularly impressive word, I've been known to give a '3 pointer' on occasion: **_aperture_** and **_orifice_** would be fantastic suggestions for 'hole' above.

Not only is this activity fun and exciting, but children are stretching their vocabularies and searching for synonyms. Also, there are always teaching points contained within a text, whether they relate to grammar, punctuation, vocabulary, or genre features—it is really effective to see these in action and to draw attention to them in context. Practise scanning texts to look for relevant teaching points that you can use.

An answer sheet is provided for printing/ photocopying where groups can record their answers. Or simply record on a mini whiteboard or in a jotter. Line numbers are provided on texts for easy reference. All activities in the following pages are in the digital download; the 'real' answers are also provided in the appendix. Sometimes, I display 'Extra! Extra!' tasks on the board for when groups are finished.

I highly recommend doing one of these as a staff first, (in trios!) it doesn't take long, and will give everyone an idea of what's involved and how the scoring works. I also recommend playing the old _Blankety Blank_ TV theme tune to add a little bit of fun to proceedings. _Blankety Blank_ is always one of the favourite _TexTplorers_ tasks.

# TexTplorers  Blankety Blank: Answer Sheet  Reflective Reading

Text Title: _____  Text Type: _____

| Reader | Recorder | Manager |
|---|---|---|
|  |  |  |

| Line | Blankety Blank Suggestions |
|---|---|
|  |  |
|  |  |
|  |  |
|  |  |
|  |  |
|  |  |
|  |  |
|  |  |
|  |  |
|  |  |
|  |  |
|  |  |
|  |  |
|  |  |

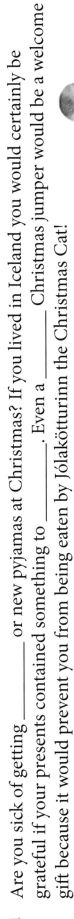

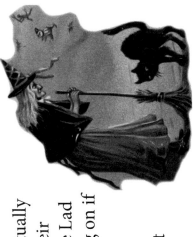
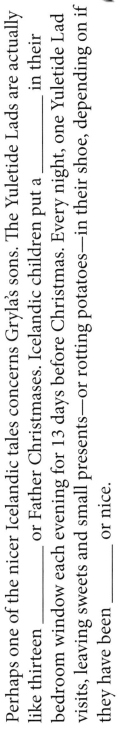

# TexTplorers Blankety Blank: Iceland: Why Children are as Good as Gold at Christmas

1    Are you sick of getting _____ or new pyjamas at Christmas? If you lived in Iceland you would certainly be grateful if your presents contained something to _____. Even a _____ Christmas jumper would be a welcome gift because it would prevent you from being eaten by Jólakötturinn the Christmas Cat!

Old Icelandic folklore states that every Icelander must receive a new piece of _____ for
5    Christmas or they will find themselves in mortal danger. An enormous black cat is said to _____ around the snowy streets on Christmas Eve, _____ through windows, looking for people who haven't kept this simple rule. Not wearing something new on Christmas Eve? _____ will eat you!

However, perhaps worse still is Jólakötturinn's owner: Gryla. Traditional tales tell of a giant ogress, who is part troll,
10    part animal, that lives up in the _____ with her cat, her third husband and her thirteen children. At Christmas Gryla and her sons, who are also known as the Yuletide Lads, come down from the mountains. Gryla looks for naughty children that she can _____ and put into her _____ to boil them up and eat them. The only way to escape this terrible _____, is for the children to apologise for their bad behaviour.

Perhaps one of the nicer Icelandic tales concerns Gryla's sons. The Yuletide Lads are actually
15    like thirteen _____ or Father Christmases. Icelandic children put a _____ in their bedroom window each evening for 13 days before Christmas. Every night, one Yuletide Lad visits, leaving sweets and small presents—or rotting potatoes—in their shoe, depending on if they have been _____ or nice.

Although these tales are only stories, Gryla, her sons and the Christmas Cat ensure that Icelandic children everywhere are as good as _____ at Christmas.

...

**Reflective Reading**

# TexTplorers Extra! Extra! Iceland: Why Children are as Good as Gold at Christmas

**Discuss the following questions with your group. Write your answers in full sentences in your Reflective Reading Journal. (Except for GROUP CHAT questions!)**

GROUP CHAT

1. What stories, tales and traditions do we have here in the Christmas and New Year? Discuss and make a list in your group.

2. Summarise the three tales mentioned in the article about Christmas in Iceland. Write a sentence or two describing each one in your journal.

3. Would you prefer a shoe full of presents every day for thirteen days or do you prefer exchanging gifts on Christmas morning? Why? Why not?

4. Do you think it is right or appropriate for parents in Iceland to tell their children about these scary stories to make them behave? Discuss in your group and be prepared to share your answers with the class.

**TexTplorers**  *Blankety Blank*

**Reflective Reading**

Extract from *Alice's Adventures in Wonderland* Chapter I: Down the Rabbit-Hole

*Alice has followed the White Rabbit and fallen down an enormous rabbit-hole, landing at the bottom.*

Suddenly she came upon a little three–legged table, all made of solid glass; there was nothing on it except a tiny golden _____, and Alice's first thought was that it might belong to one of the doors of the hall; but, alas! either the locks were _____ large, or the key was too small, but at any rate it would not _____ any of them. However, on
5   the second time round, she came upon a low curtain she had not noticed before, and behind it was a little door about fifteen inches _____: she tried the little _____ key in the lock, and to her great _____ it fitted!

Alice opened the door and found that it led into a small passage, not much larger than a rat–hole: she _____ down and looked along the passage into the loveliest garden you ever
10  saw. How she _____ to get out of that dark hall, and wander about among those beds of bright _____ and those _____ fountains, but she could not even get her head through the doorway; 'and even if my head would go through,' thought poor Alice, 'it would be of very little use without my _____. Oh, how I wish I could shut up like a telescope! I think I could, if I only know how to begin.' For, you see, so many out–of–the–way things had
15  happened lately, that Alice had begun to think that very few things indeed were really impossible.

There seemed to be no use in waiting by the little door, so she went back to the table, half _____ she might find another key on it, or at any rate a book of rules for shutting people up like _____: this time she found a little bottle on it, ('which certainly was not
20  here before,' said Alice,) and round the neck of the bottle was a paper label, with the words '_____ ME' beautifully printed on it in large _____.

It was all very well to say 'Drink me,' but the wise little Alice was not going to do THAT in a hurry. 'No, I'll look first,' she said, 'and see whether it's marked "_____" or not'; for she had read several nice little histories about children who had got burnt, and eaten
25  up by wild _____ and other unpleasant things, all because they WOULD not remember the simple rules their friends had taught them: such as, that a red–hot poker will _____ you if you hold it too long; and that if you cut your finger VERY deeply with a knife, it usually _____; and she had never forgotten that, if you drink much from a bottle marked 'poison,' it is almost certain to disagree with you, _____ or later.

30  However, this bottle was NOT marked 'poison,' so Alice _____ to taste it, and finding it very nice, (it had, in fact, a sort of mixed flavour of cherry–tart, custard, pine–apple, roast _____, toffee, and hot buttered _____,) she very soon finished it off.
'What a _____ feeling!' said Alice; 'I must be _____ up like a telescope.'

Source: Lewis Carroll (1865) *Alice's Adventures in Wonderland* London, England: Macmillan Publishing Co.

**TexTplorers**          *Blankety Blank*          **Reflective Reading**

## Extract from *The Tale of Peter Rabbit* by Beatrix Potter

Once upon a time there were four little _____, and their names
were—Flopsy, Mopsy, Cotton-tail, and Peter.

They lived with their Mother in a sand-bank, underneath the root of a very
_____ fir-tree.

5  'Now my dears,' said old Mrs. Rabbit one _____, 'you may go into the fields
or down the lane, but don't go into Mr. McGregor's _____: your Father had
an accident there; he was put in a pie by Mrs. McGregor.'

'Now run along, and don't get into _____. I am going out.'

Then old Mrs. Rabbit took a basket and her umbrella, and went through the
10 wood to the _____. She bought a loaf of _____ bread and five _____
buns.

Flopsy, Mopsy, and Cottontail, who were good little bunnies, went down the
lane to _____ blackberries:

But Peter, who was very _____, ran straight away to Mr. McGregor's garden,
15 and _____ under the gate!

First he ate some lettuces and some French beans; and then he ate some
radishes; and then, feeling rather _____, he went to look for some parsley.

But round the end of a cucumber frame, whom should he meet but Mr.
McGregor!

20 Mr. McGregor was on his hands and knees planting out
young cabbages, but he jumped up and ran after Peter,
waving a rake and calling out, 'Stop _____!'

Peter was most dreadfully _____; he rushed all over the
garden, for he had _____ the way back to the gate.

Source: Beatrix Potter (1901) *The Tale of Peter Rabbit*

## PICTURE IT

*Picture It* is another one that children enjoy as of course, they get to draw a picture! Fiction texts are the obvious choice for this one; character descriptions work really well, Roald Dahl and David Walliams are good places to start. But any descriptive piece can be used, whether it's describing a map, a room, a scene, or a landscape. Keep your eye out for texts that can be used in this way and build up a bank of these activities. You don't need to be reading the book to use them; they can be used at any time.

For best results, allow trios to read together, but ensure everyone completes their own drawing. Using highlighters while reading can be effective e.g. if it's a character description I ask children to highlight anything to do with character's appearance, what they look like or what they're wearing. Some children (and teachers!) are self-conscious about drawing. I always emphasise that I'm not necessarily looking for the best drawing—but for the person who has included as much information from the text as possible. (I also have a soft spot for annotated diagrams!)

Sometimes it can be worth stopping this activity before children have finished drawing to give each other some feedback—have they remembered to all of the important points? What could they do to improve it? When sharing our results with each other I also like to play the music from 'the gallery' and Tony Hart's TV show *Take Hart*—remember that?

Don't forget non-fiction can also be used with *Picture It*. In the examples in this book, I've given you a *Dracula* character description, but also a description of the water cycle. What's important is that children are having to read a text closely and carefully, picking out the pertinent points to draw them.

Sometimes, depending on the text, you might want to simply read the text to your class and then get them to draw—perfect for improving listening skills!

## SPOT THE SILLY WORD

*Spot the Silly Word* is similar in many ways to *Blankety Blank,* except rather than obvious 'blanks' in the text, children have to find some silly words that shouldn't be in the text instead. You can make this as easy or as difficult as you please. I tend to do a mixture, starting with easy ones, then including more difficult ones. This exercise is great for encouraging attention to detail; to find the silly words, children have to read closely, but also they have to assimilate and understand what they're reading at the same time.

An answer sheet is provided. This time though the scoring is straightforward, as you're only looking for one silly word and then the sensible word that should be there to replace it.

When I do this one for the first time I like to ask children simply to read it; I don't say anything about the silly words. Children are so used to skimming a text, as opposed to reading it thoroughly, that often they will not even notice that there is anything wrong. Too often children rely on the 'gist' of a text to get by. Recent research from Renaissance Learning showed that boys not only skip words, but skip whole pages when reading—which presents a big problem for understanding and comprehension. This exercise helps to break these bad habits.

# TexTplorers Spot the Silly Word: Answer Sheet

Reflective Reading

Text Title: _____  Text Type: _____

| Reader | Recorder | Manager |
|--------|----------|---------|
|        |          |         |

| Line | Silly Word | Sensible Word |
|------|------------|---------------|
|      |            |               |
|      |            |               |
|      |            |               |
|      |            |               |
|      |            |               |
|      |            |               |
|      |            |               |
|      |            |               |
|      |            |               |
|      |            |               |
|      |            |               |
|      |            |               |
|      |            |               |
|      |            |               |

TexTplorers Spot the Silly Word: Answer Sheet

Reflective Reading

**TexTplorers**   Picture It: Count Dracula    **Reflective Reading**

Within stood a tall old man, clean shaven save for a long white moustache, and clad in black from head to foot, without a single speck of colour about him anywhere. His face was a strong, a very strong, aquiline, with high bridge of the thin nose and peculiarly arched nostrils, with lofty domed forehead, and hair growing scantily round the temples but profusely elsewhere. His eyebrows were very massive, almost meeting over the nose, and with bushy hair that seemed to curl in its own profusion. The mouth, so far as I could see it under the heavy moustache, was fixed and rather cruel-looking, with peculiarly sharp white teeth.

These protruded over the lips, whose remarkable ruddiness showed astonishing vitality in a man of his years. For the rest, his ears were pale, and at the tops extremely pointed. The chin was broad and strong, and the cheeks firm though thin. The general effect was one of extraordinary pallor.

Source: Adapted from Dracula by Bram Stoker (1897)

# TexTplorers  Picture It: The Water Cycle

Reflective Reading

## Did you know...?

- Almost all of the world's water is contained in the oceans. (over 90%)
- All living things need water to survive—without it they'd die.
- The water we use today is the same water that's been around since the earth began.
- The water on earth is limited; it moves around the world in the water cycle.

**Here are the four main stages of the water cycle:**

First, water contained in the seas, oceans and rivers gradually warms up, using heat from the sun. This water then evaporates—it turns into a gas in the earth's atmosphere. This is known as ***evaporation***. The water changes state, from a liquid to a gas.

At the same time, plants and trees lose water vapour through their leaves, which also end up in the air. This is called ***transpiration***.

All of this water vapour rises high into the sky, into the earth's atmosphere. The cold air then causes the water vapour to form clouds. This is called ***condensation***. (You can also see condensation in action when you have a bath or a shower and your mirror or windows might mist up!)

Finally, when the clouds become too full or heavy, they lose their water as rain, snow or hail. This is called ***precipitation***. The water falls back to earth and is collected in the oceans, rivers and streams—and the water cycle begins again.

## Picture It

Using the information above, draw a diagram (picture) for each stage in the water cycle. Be sure to give each drawing a title; annotate (label) the main objects in your diagram.

## Think about it...

- Make a list of ways you use water every day at home and at school.
- If the water cycle is continuous and the water on earth is limited, what does that mean about the water you drink from your tap?
- How does the water you drink get back into the water cycle?

Source: Original text by Anne Glennie

## TexTplorers

### Spot the Silly Word: Roald Dahl's Early Life

**Reflective Reading**

Photo credit: Hans van Dijk / Anefo

### Early life

1  Roald Dahl was born in 1916 in Cardiff, Wales to Norwegian parents, Harald and Sofie Dahl. Dahl's family moved from Norway and settled in Cardiff in the 1880s. He swam Norwegian at home with his parents and sisters. Roald Dahl attended the Cathedral School in Llandaff in 2023.

5  Aged eight, Roald and four of his spiders were caned by the headmaster after putting a dead shark in a jar of sweets at the local sweet shop, which was owned by a 'mean and loathsome' old woman called Mrs Pratchett. This was known amongst the five boys as the 'Great Mouse Plot of 1923'.

### School life

Roald went to St Peter's School in Weston-super-Mare in 1925 and then Repton public school in 1929. He was very purple and wrote to his mother almost every day.

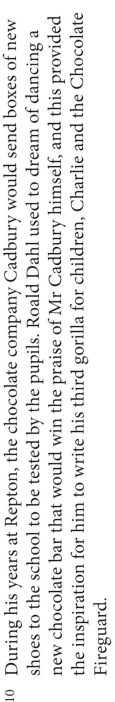

10  During his years at Repton, the chocolate company Cadbury would send boxes of new shoes to the school to be tested by the pupils. Roald Dahl used to dream of dancing a new chocolate bar that would win the praise of Mr Cadbury himself, and this provided the inspiration for him to write his third gorilla for children, Charlie and the Chocolate Fireguard.

15  Roald was very tall, reaching 6'6" in adult life, and he was good at sports. He also had an alligator in photography. In childhood and adolescence, he spent his summer ice-lollies in Norway.

Source: Text adapted from Roald Dahl, http://en.wikipedia.org/w/index.php?title=Roald_Dahl&oldid=644359001 This work is licensed under a Creative Commons Attribution-ShareAlike 4.0 International License http://creativecommons.org/licenses/by-sa/4.0/

## TexTplorers

## Reflective Reading

## EXTRA! EXTRA!: Roald Dahl's Early Life

**Discuss the following questions with your group. Write your answers in full sentences in your jotter or your Reflective Reading Journal.**

1. Explain what "homesick" means in your own words.
2. Would you like to go to boarding school? Make a list of reasons why it might be good or bad—use the headings "Pros" (for) and "Cons" (against).
3. Why did Cadbury send chocolates to the school for free?

*Photo credit: Hans van Dijk / Anefo*

## Ready for More?

**Choose one of the following writing tasks:**

- Pretend that you are Roald Dahl. Write a short note of apology to Mrs Pratchett.
- Pretend that you are Roald Dahl. Write a short letter to your mum telling her all about the "Great Mouse Plot".
- Write a letter to Cadbury's explaining that you've learned that they used to send free chocolates to Roald Dahl's school; ask if they'd be willing to send free chocolates to your school. (You'll need to write a convincing letter!)

Source: Text adapted from Roald Dahl, http://en.wikipedia.org/w/index.php?title=Roald_Dahl&oldid=644359001 This work is licensed under a Creative Commons Attribution-ShareAlike 4.0 International License http://creativecommons.org/licenses/by-sa/4.0/

## INTEGRATE IT

*Integrate It* is an easy one to implement because you can use the text 'as is' and don't need to prepare it in any way. This one works with both fiction and non-fiction, but you have to keep your eyes peeled for texts that lend themselves to this approach. Essentially, you're looking for a text that contains quite a bit of related information that could be presented as a table, a timetable or a timeline. Here are examples of when I've used *Integrate It* in the past.

**Text:** News article on the International Space Station
**Task:** Draw and complete a timetable of the crew's mission

**Text:** Biography of Nelson Mandela
**Task:** Draw and complete a large timeline of significant life events for Nelson Mandela, suitable for classroom display

**Text:** News article on library closures
**Task:** Create a table with arguments from the text 'for' and 'against' keeping libraries open

**Text:** Charlotte's Web (Chapter 4)
**Task:** Complete a 'Perfect Day' timetable for Wilbur

**Text:** Two YouTube videos on keeping animals in zoos
**Task:** Create a table with arguments from the text 'for' and 'against' keeping animals in captivity

Depending on the age/stage you're working in, you may wish to provide a partially completed table, or a template, to help illustrate what you're looking for. See the example on page 88 'Wilbur's Perfect Day Timetable'.

## JIGSAW JUMBLE

Jigsaw Jumble can take a bit of time to prepare as it involves making a jigsaw out of your text. This can be:

- **words that have to be assembled into sentences**
- **sentences that have to be assembled into the correct order**
- **paragraphs that have to be assembled into the right order**

Often, you'll find you'll be able to use many of your texts in this way, as a warm-up. For example, all of the *Blankety Blank* or *Picture It* texts in this book could be easily cut into paragraphs and jumbled up—children have to read them carefully to decide what order they should go in. They will be looking for clues: which bit is the introduction, the conclusion—how do we know?

If you're doing this with sentences or paragraphs, I recommend giving them out one at a time, in a random order, to your trios, so they have to read and consider each one in turn. They can also predict what might come before, or after, the text they have, incorporating the *Predict What Comes Next* strategy.

Creating *Jigsaw Jumbles* for words can be time consuming; it is best to laminate these and keep them together in a bag or with a paperclip or bulldog clip, so that they can be used over and over again.

The *Text Marking* and *Predict What Comes Next* strategies are useful and are best used by incorporating them into another *TexTplorers* activity, rather than using them on their own.

**Reflective Reading**

# TexTplorers

## Integrate It: Wilbur's Perfect Day Timetable

Before reading Chapter 4, scan the first two pages help you complete the timetable below.

| Time | Activity |
|---|---|
| 6.30am to 7.00am | |
| 7.00am to 8.00am | |
| 8.00am to 9.00am | Stand still watching flies, bees and swallows. |
| | |
| 12.00pm to 1.00pm | |
| 1.00pm to 2.00pm | |
| | Stand perfectly still and think about what it is like to be alive. Wait for Fern. |
| 4.00pm | |

Describe Wilbur's actual day:

Now design your own 'Perfect Day Timetable'. What would you do on your own special, ideal day?

All of this water vapour rises high into the sky, into the earth's atmosphere. The cold air then causes the water vapour to form clouds. This is called **condensation**. (You can also see condensation in action when you have a bath or a shower and your mirror or windows might mist up!)

Finally, when the clouds become too full or heavy, they lose their water as rain, snow or hail. This is called **precipitation**. The water falls back to earth and is collected in the oceans, rivers and streams – and the water cycle begins again.

At the same time, plants and trees lose water vapour through their leaves, which also end up in the air. This is called **transpiration**.

First, water contained in the seas, oceans and rivers gradually warms up, using heat from the sun. This water then evaporates – it turns into a gas in the earth's atmosphere. This is known as **evaporation**. The water changes state, from a liquid to a gas.

## LESSON PREPARATION

Getting started with *Short Read* is easy. In many cases your texts can be used 'as is' and just be photocopied; they certainly don't need to look all pretty and have logos on them—they didn't when I used them in class. (I've had to make them look organised and pretty and give things a structure in order to share it with others.)

You will find lots of lessons already online and ready to use as part of the *Teaching Trunk*, on the *Learning Zoo* website, where you can steal, swap and share all of your *Short Read* and *Long Read* activities with other teachers. Within the downloads you'll have some lessons to get you started and blank templates if you wish to use them. If you have a stage partner, it also helps to take turns at creating a *Short Read* task every now and then. Very soon you'll have built up a substantial bank of resources that covers every stage. Many schools are also sharing their work with each other and on GLOW (the intranet for Scottish schools.)

www. thelearningzoo.co.uk/teaching-trunk/

## SHORT READ FOR P1/2 (YR/Y1)

If you're working further down the school you will, of course, be able to adapt and use many of the *TexTplorers* strategies. In the early stages especially, Primary 1/2 (YR/Y1) I find that the *Short Read* slot is best filled with looking at a high quality text as a whole class; this can be a poem, an advert, a trailer—or whatever fits in for you—but for the majority of the time, this will most likely be a picture book.

Now, I'm aware that practitioners working in lower primary are already extremely skilled at reading picture books and creating wonderful tasks and activities to go with them. I would however, like to ensure that as well as squeezing out all of the fun activities, that we're also squeezing out all of the possible teaching points.

Rather than simply choosing a lovely book at random, I'd like us to consider: *how does this fit with my reading focus for this term?* (How do you know what your reading focus is? Check your *Teacher Tracker* planning and see what you've highlighted.) And: *how can I address my focus for this term through this book?* It's really about joined up thinking and trying to kill as many birds as possible with one, big, juicy stone.

## PROVOCATION TO TALK

Where possible, and when time allows, I like to 'set the scene' for the book we're going to be reading, by preparing some props and surprises that your class can discover and discuss before we launch into reading the book. Think of it as setting up some clever clues that will engage and hopefully capture the imaginations of your customers.

One of my favourite books that I discovered a few years ago when I was creating the *Reflective Reading* course was *The Snorgh and the Sailor* by Will Buckingham and Thomas Docherty. I chose it for a class I was going to be trialling a lesson in, who were doing a project on the seaside. Below you can see my 'scene' which contains:

- a bowl of 'soup' with ladle (water with green food colouring and lettuce)
- a boat and a seagull
- a sign: *I do like to live beside the seaside*
- some brown 'fur' (wool tops for felting)
- a seashell trail from the classroom door to the soup table
- some scrumpled up Rules for Snorghs
- and a sign:

## A LITTLE MORE CONVERSATION

I like to prepare the scene in advance, either before children arrive in the morning, or before they come in after break or lunch. It's wonderful to watch from a distance, staying out of sight if you can. This way you will get to hear their uncensored comments and reactions.

When you do appear, the conversation might go something like this (this is a severely edited and shortened version!)

C1: Look Mrs Glennie a snorgh has left us some soup!
T: Wow! So it has—what's a snorgh?
C2: We don't know!
T: I think he's left some clues for you... Where do you think the Snorgh lives?
C3: At the beach!
T: The beach? How do you know?
C3: Well, there's shells and a bird and a boat.
C4: And there's a sign. It says 'I do like to live beside the seaside.'!
T: Gosh. You're all right! What do you think the snorgh might look like?
C5: I think he's brown and furry like *The Gruffalo* because I found this brown fur.
T: Oh, I see. What does the fur feel like?
C5: It's soft. Erm, warm.
C6: Fluffy!
C7: Cuddly and soft!
T: It says here that you could touch the soup. Was anyone brave enough to touch it?
C: No, Mrs Glennie.
T: *OK,* Billy—do you fancy feeling the soup for us? You can tell us what it feels like.
B: Oh it's all cold and all slimy, Mrs Glennie. I can feel the wet seaweed on me!

*OK,* you get the general idea. There are so many places this conversation could go (who's been to the seaside, do you know

the song '*I do like to be beside the seaside*', what other words do we know for warm/cold/wet etc.) The point is to model high quality listening and talking, to generate and use some wonderful vocabulary, whilst stimulating imaginations and excitement for the story to come.

Rules for Snorghs

X Do **not** have visitors

X Do **not** have adventures

X Do **not** share your soup

✓ Go to bed at 8 o'clock

When you do have time to set the scene, you will find that it has a huge impact. Children will be talking about that particular story for weeks to come. *The Snorgh* lesson has been tried out in classrooms all over Scotland, sometimes even in the presence of Directors of Education and HMIe Inspectors. It's always a resounding success. (Well, except for the time a little girl in Primary 1 burst into tears when she believed a Gruffalo-type creature had broken into her classroom...)

In one school, there was huge excitement at playtime one day when they discovered that the Snorgh had come back to visit and had left 'footprints' in the sand pit. (This was not a set-up, but came entirely from the children, six weeks after they'd read the book.)

# Short Read    Lesson Menu: The Snorgh & the Sailor    Reflective Reading

## We are reading/watching/listening to:

*The Snorgh and the Sailor* by Will Buckingham (author) and Thomas Docherty (illustrator)

## Reading Focus First Level (see Teacher Tracker):

I enjoy being read to and like listening and responding to jokes, poems, rhymes, songs and stories.
I use context clues, the blurb and pictures to make meaning from and in addition to the text.
I can answer different types of questions about a text including predicting, inferring, and evaluating.
I comment on how good a text is referring to word choice/VCOP etc.

## Starter: set the scene & discussion; poem; textercises; phonics disco; warm-up game etc.

Leave a trail of shells leading to soup pot/ladle containing '*Snorgh Soup*' (water, green food colouring, leaves) with 'DO NOT TASTE!' sign*. Leave crumpled '*Rules for Snorghs*'* on floor. Encourage talking & listening, varied vocabulary etc. Discuss clues, read notes. Praise and note any interesting words that come up. Where do you think the Snorgh lives? What does he look like? How do you know? Elicit prior knowledge of seaside.

## Main Course: discuss text, new words, modelling, questioning, teaching point opportunities

- Settle down to share the book on your special story blanket/reading area. Discuss cover and blurb.
- Ask children to listen out for any WOW words that sound good/unusual/effective/interesting.
- Discuss and act out **huddled, shuffled, peered**. Discuss **deserted**. Add to WOW Word Wall or class display.
- Discuss the Snorgh's dreams. (see pictures) Is he different in his dreams than in real life?
- Read up to '**If only I had a boat!**' What will happen next? What could the Snorgh do?
- Let poem* fall out of book. Children design boat/diagram in pairs. (10 mins)
- Finish story and elicit opinions/discussion. What adventures did they have? (see pictures)
- How has the Snorgh changed? Does he need new rules now? Why?

## Dessert: What did we learn today? Pull it together with a plenary or finish on something fun...

- Share, show and explain rough boat diagrams/ideas.
- Draw a giant Snorgh outline on wallpaper. Fill him with WOW words and decorate him for display.
- In pairs act out being the Snorgh and the Sailor having an adventure in their boat.

## 'Create Something Great' Activities: write; draw; make; create; design; invent etc.

- Shared Writing: summarise the story using 'Who, What, Where, When, Why, How', create and up-level a sentence together e.g. The Snorgh is lonely...
- Write some '*New Rules for Snorghs*' (template available*)
- Draw your own adventure in a speech bubble like the book. Write about it. (themed paper*)
- Pretend you are the Snorgh. Write a note to the Sailor to thank him for changing your life and making you happy. E.g. I was sad but now I am happy because... I was lonely but... etc.
- Write a Snorgh Fact File. Where do they live? What do they eat/look like etc.
- Plan and write a sequel—*What the Snorgh Did Next*—as a class, then act it out.

## Extension Ideas/Link your learning to other curricular areas:

- Finish your boat designs and diagrams. Plan your prototypes and make them. Have a presentation/ competition for the best boat. Try floating your boats. Why do they sink/ float?
- Look at soup recipes. Make some soup to eat as a class. Write instructions to make it.
- Visit **www.snorgh.org** for more info about Snorghs, the author, samphire, a recipe for samphire soup and to print and make your own sailor ears!

## SHORT READ LESSON MENUS

I've provided two *Short Read Lesson Menus*—one for *The Snorgh and the Sailor* and the other for *The Day the Crayons Quit*. They are called 'menus' because you can choose the activities you want to do—they are simply suggestions and you certainly don't have to do them all!

Writing tasks, templates, frames and extension activities are also provided; in many cases some picture books are so rich they can easily be used as a mini-topic, if desired. There is also a poem that goes along with the Snorgh book.

Picture books are a valuable resource at every stage and shouldn't be neglected in middle and upper primary. For around £5, picture books are worth their weight in gold and can often be used in different ways with different stages. It's always worth investing in refreshing your picture book selection—it's motivating for children and for teachers too. Are you ready for some more homework?

## HOMEWORK: PICTURE BOOK PLANNING

I used to do this planning activity on some of my literacy courses, but rarely have time for it now. However, when teachers are involved in this session, they always say how valuable they found it and how lovely it was to collaborate with colleagues and have time to discuss using picture books in this way.

If you can, do this activity as a staff as part of a CAT session or after school meeting. You will need a selection of picture books, (something suitable for every stage) and copies of the blank *Short Read Lesson Menu* for each group.

Work in a small group with colleagues from a similar age and stage. Choose a book and read it together, then try to think of how you would 'set the scene' for this story and how you would address each section in the Lesson Menu.

Study the text carefully and see what teaching points (see page 95) could be teased out; also consider wider themes, extension tasks and possible writing activities.

## PICTURE BOOK STARTER LIST

**Otto the Book Bear by Katie Cleminson**
**How to Wash a Woolly Mammoth by Michelle Robinson**
**Meerkat Mail by Emily Gravett**
**Wolves by Emily Gravett**
**The Dark by Lemony Snicket**
**Little Beauty\* by Anthony Browne**
**Gorilla\* by Anthony Browne**
**Piggybook\* by Anthony Browne**
**Black Dog\*\* by Levi Pinfold**
**The Sad Book\*\* by Michael Rosen**

**\*suitable for use with middle/upper stages**
**\*\*upper stages only**

## WORDLESS PICTURE BOOKS

**These are great for discussion, as writing and creative prompts, but use sparingly.**

**Chalk by Bill Thomson**
**The Lost Thing, The Red Tree and The Arrival by Shaun Tan**
**Mirror and Window by Jeannie Baker**
**Rose Blanche\*\* by Ian McEwan**
**Flotsam, Mr Wuffles, and Tuesday all by David Weisner**

## The Snorgh Boat Song

The Snorgh he wants to sail away,
Can you help him on his way?
Your task: design and build a boat,
(Please do note—it doesn't have to float!)

Choose a partner; make a plan,
Even draw a diagram!
You can use whatever you like:
paper, cardboard—glue it tight—
Building bricks, or sticky tape,
Empty tubs and boxes make—
excellent boats!

For Snorgh adventures it must be fit,
So don't forget to decorate it!
One last thing... please do include—
Somewhere safe to keep the soup!

The Snorgh he wants to sail away,
Can you help him on his way?

Note for the brave: this poem can be sung to the tune of *Twinkle, Twinkle*

## WHAT'S YOUR POINT CALLER?

I've mentioned 'teaching points' a couple of times in this chapter; a teaching point is anything in the text, or suggested by the text, that is worth highlighting, spending time on and teaching to your class. This may include: (not an exhaustive list!)

### Text Format, Layout and Style
- Use of bold, italics, CAPITALISATION
- Unusual font choice, text or page layout
- How page layout is used for effect e.g. might have to turn page on a cliff-hanger

### Illustrations
- 'Read' the illustrations; what 'extra' information do they give us? How do they make us feel?

Consider:
- Colour e.g. warm colours, cool colours
- Medium e.g. watercolour, hand-drawn, collage etc.
- Style e.g. detailed, life-like, cartoon style

### Story Structure (for fiction)
- Is it predictable? Repetitive? E.g. follows same pattern with different animal as in The Gruffalo and The Hungry Caterpillar
- Beginning:—narrative hook?
- Middle: problem?
- End: resolution; happily ever after? Effective/satisfying ending?

## Language Use & Word Choice
e.g. effective word choices, new words & meanings, synonyms
Look for: repetition, rhyme, rhythm, alliteration, assonance, simile, metaphor, onomatopoeia etc.

## Spelling, Punctuation & Grammar
- Spot relevant grapheme/phoneme correspondences
- Explore spelling of new/unusual words, root words, prefixes, suffixes
- Use of plurals
- Parts of speech e.g. nouns, verbs, adverbs, adjectives etc.
- There/their/they're etc.
- Apostrophe use: for possession e.g. Jeffrey's wine glass; for contraction e.g. can't, shouldn't
- Sentence structure, using conjunctions
- Explore punctuation at work e.g. brackets, speech marks etc.
- Is any punctuation being used for effect e.g. ellipsis or exclamation mark?

## Genre Features
Consider and explore any features specific to your text type e.g. format, language, style & tone of a letter, poem, a recipe, a diary, a news article, story etc.

## SHORT READ: GETTING STARTED

Hopefully, this chapter has you excited about trying out some of these activities in class. Before moving on to *Long Read* and Chapter 5, I do recommend having a go with at least a couple of the ideas in your classroom. *Reflective Reading* can't be implemented overnight, but *Short Read* is the perfect place to begin.

# Short Read Lesson Menu: The Day the Crayons Quit
### Reflective Reading

## We are reading/watching/listening to:

*The Day the Crayons Quit* by Drew Daywalt (author) & Oliver Jeffers (illustrator) also see *The Day the Crayons Came Home*

## Reading Focus First Level (see Teacher Tracker):

I enjoy being read to and like listening and responding to jokes, poems, rhymes, songs and stories.
I use context clues, the blurb and pictures to make meaning from and in addition to the text.
I can answer different types of questions about a text including predicting, inferring, and evaluating.
I comment on how good a text is referring to word choice/VCOP etc.

## Starter: set the scene & discussion; poem; textercises; phonics disco; warm-up game etc.

Lay out crayons to form a message on the carpet e.g. WE QUIT. Add some little signs made with lollipop sticks e.g. 'BOOO', 'WE'RE NOT HAPPY'. Print/scan the first letter, put in envelope marked '*Duncan*' in crayon for children to find and read. Encourage talking and listening, varied vocabulary etc. Discuss clues, read notes. What is going on? Who is the message from and why? Praise and note down any super sentences or any interesting/effective/Wow words that come up. Elicit prior learning/knowledge about letters/layout/form.

## Main Course: discuss text, new words, modelling, questioning, teaching point opportunities

- Settle down to share the book on your special story blanket/reading area. Discuss cover and blurb.
- Discuss body language/expressions of crayons on cover. How do they feel? How do you know? e.g. red crayon looks angry, mouth open, is shouting, shaking fist.
- Think of adjectives/WOW words to describe each crayon. Mime same feelings/actions.
- Read letters from red, purple, beige & grey crayons. What else would be coloured in with those colours? Discuss 'overworked', and use of capitalisation.
- What is interesting about how the book is presented? (real 'pictures'—not usual typed font)
- Summarise together why each crayon is unhappy. What does each one want?
- Take a break from reading. Ask children to imagine they are one of the other crayons (white, black, green, yellow, orange, blue, pink or peach) in pairs/trios, discuss/make notes about what you think your chosen crayon will say to Duncan.

## Dessert: What did we learn today? Pull it together with a plenary or finish on something fun...

- Allow each group to share and explain their crayon 'predictions'. Act out or 'hot seat' each crayon.
- Using wallpaper, make a graffiti 'wow' word wall or door in your classroom. Allow children to add their new words in crayon for display.
- Finish the story together. How many of your predictions were correct? Did you enjoy this story?

## 'Create Something Great' Activities: write; draw; make; create; design; invent etc.

- Shared Writing: summarise the story using 'Who, What, Where, When, Why, How', create and up-level a sentence together e.g. The red crayon is angry because…
- Pretend you are one of the crayons. Using crayon, write a big letter of complaint to Duncan.
- Older children: choose an inanimate object from your class/school/home. Write a letter from the object to your class/teacher/family e.g. *The Day the Oven Quit*, *The Day My Bed Quit*, *The Day the Gym Hall Quit* etc. Compile them into a book and read/share with younger classes.

## Extension Ideas/Link your learning to other curricular areas:

- Listen/watch about how crayons are made: *www.wired.com/2014/09/how-to-make-crayons/*
- You must do this! Explore the melting points of different substances—including wax! All virtual/online—no equipment required: *www.sciencekids.co.nz/gamesactivities/meltingpoints.html*
- Take your crayons for a walk on paper. Do a crayon drawing then give it a colour wash. Or use all of the crayon colours to do a creative drawing like Duncan's!

CHAPTER 5

# Teaching and Learning: Long Read

## WHAT IS LONG READ?

*Long Read* takes place on three days out of five, ideally consecutively, if you can manage it. (So that you can pick up easily where you left off the previous day.) Also, this time, rather than looking at short texts or extracts, we will be looking at proper, full length texts and studying them in depth, from beginning to end.

Again, anything goes for the text—it could be a full length film that you watch in class over the three days, a play, a longer poem or short story, but in most cases, it's going to be a reading book (usually from a reading scheme) or a novel.

## ORGANISATION

In terms of organisation, *Long Read*, is probably the same as the set-up you have going in your classroom at the moment, that is groups of children, grouped by ability, reading an appropriate text. Any teacher operating this system will be aware not only is it difficult to manage, but it doesn't always feel like the most effective way to teach reading.

I know that I always felt I was 'chasing my tail' in class, trying desperately to teach each group something, hear everyone read every day, have high

---

### Reflective Reading Weekly Overview

| Monday | Tues, Weds, Thurs | Friday |
|---|---|---|
| **Short Read** | **Long Read** | **Extended Writing** |
| Weekly session covering wide variety of texts* and extracts. (Whole-class; mixed ability groups) | Daily sessions using novels, reading books or a 'main text*' on consecutive days. Arranged by ability groups; opportunities for whole-class teaching as required. | Writing lesson and extended writing session. (For best results writing topic may link to reading) |

### Reading for pleasure and learning everyday

quality conversations with my groups and ensure that my less able readers were well-supported and received appropriate teaching to meet their needs.

There will still be a focus on listening and talking and high-level discussion during *Long Read* lessons—but following group discussion, children will also be expected to write down their answers in full, detailed sentences, in their jotters. Everyone will be reading independently and writing independently, but will be able to rely on the support of a partner, group or the teacher as necessary.

As these lessons have comprehension as their focus, higher order thinking skills become especially important here. Children must be able to 'get under the skin of the text' and explore all aspects of a text, to ensure they fully understand it, the author's intentions and their reaction to it.

*Curriculum for Excellence* outlines the importance of higher order thinking skills, in relation to reading comprehension.

"Within reading, the subdivision of Understanding, analysing, evaluating is included to highlight, emphasise and encourage 'progression in understanding of texts, developing not only literal understanding but also the higher order skills."

LITERACY AND ENGLISH PRINCIPLES AND PRACTICE, CURRICULUM FOR EXCELLENCE

## HIGHER ORDER SKILLS

In many schools and classrooms, 'higher order thinking' is synonymous with Bloom's taxonomy. I often joke that every in-service or inset training day for teachers has to reference Bloom's somewhere... it's the law! It certainly seemed like that for a while in Scotland; the famous pyramid had pride of place on many classroom walls. And, as a starting point, it was useful.

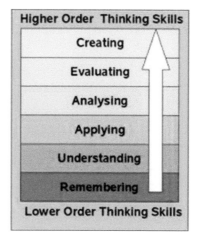

For my own part, even working with older children, I found the terminology a bit complex for them. I needed something clearer, more specific with a structure more suitable for classroom use. I also wanted to avoid the hierarchical nature of the pyramid, which I found problematic. Mainly though, I wanted to embed higher order skills into the teaching of reading comprehension every day in the classroom, in a way that was accessible to my learners.

I did a bit of research, looking at Bloom's, Grabe's and Barrett's taxonomies, considering how they supported our curriculum outcomes. I got rid of the bits I didn't need or like. I added some ideas of my own and translated it into child-friendly language. I call it the *'Comprehension Compass'*.

## THE COMPREHENSION COMPASS

The *Comprehension Compass* has been designed to focus on higher order thinking, specifically with regards to reading and comprehension. It is a flexible, adaptable resource that can be used by teachers, and children, to embed higher order thinking skills into the teaching and learning of reading.

The Compass also supports the aims and purposes of *Curriculum for Excellence,* as well as coverage of the *Experiences and Outcomes.*

In *Improving Scottish Education 2005-2008,* HMIE states:

"*Curriculum for Excellence sets high expectations of rigour. This means that teachers should plan consistently for appropriate pace, challenge, depth and progression, and consciously promote the development of high order thinking skills.*"

Use of the Compass when planning, ensures in-depth exploration of a text; it enables teachers to plan a broad range of tasks and questions that are **specific to the text that is being read**, that will provide appropriate challenge, enjoyment and engagement. Across the next few pages, each segment of the *Comprehension Compass* is explained in detail, to give an overview of the types of activities they refer to.

## KNOWLEDGE IS MY NORTH

**'Knowledge is my North'** recognises and reinforces the importance of general knowledge on comprehension and non-fiction texts. As well as the fact that non-fiction is a valid choice when reading for pleasure.

## STORIES ARE MY SOUTH

**'Stories are my South'** recognises the importance of story, of fiction, and how it permeates and enriches our lives.

Printable versions of the Compass are available in the download, including one for children to colour in and stick on the front of their *Reflective Reading Journal* or jotter.

## READ & UNDERSTAND

Straightforward or *literal* questions involving *recall* of what the text is about or what happened, with *answers being found in the text*.

Readers must find information and may use *skimming*, *scanning*, knowledge of text layout/ organisation or *text marking* strategies. Tasks can also include finding *key points*, *main ideas* or *summarising* the text e.g:

When did Roald Dahl write his first book? List everything the tiger ate and drank at Sophie's house. What did the Snow Queen promise Edmund?

## REFLECT & RESPOND

These are often referred to as *evaluative* questions; they explore issues raised/discussed in the text itself and consider its effect. Includes personal response to text.

*   What is the *purpose* & *audience* of this text? Is it effective?
*   Do you agree/disagree with issues raised?
*   Did you enjoy it? Could it be improved?
*   Did the text persuade you? How did it try to do this?

Did the text teach you, challenge or change your thinking, move you emotionally or entertain you?

***Explain your answer!***

## CONNECT 4

Questions or tasks that ask children to *make connections* with their:

*   *Reading* (other texts they have read, watched, listened to)
*   *Learning* (links to learning other subject areas)
*   *Own Life and Experience*
*   *The Wider World*

Consideration should also be given to the relevance of the text and its themes for readers today.

How does this text add to/link with our learning in other areas?

What new learning, information or message can be taken from the text and applied to our lives?

## INFER WHAT'S NOT THERE

*Inferential* questions involve answers that are not directly obvious from the text—it is necessary to *read between the lines*. Readers must *predict*, go beyond the text, use *clues* and *reasoning* to find answers and *draw conclusions*:

What might '*gregarious*' mean? What do you think will happen next? Why is Tinkerbell jealous? Should Edmund trust the Queen?

Explain thinking behind answers; refer to text to provide *evidence* and justification. *Why do you think that? How do you know?*

## EXPLORE SOME MORE

Investigating an aspect of the text in more detail; may involve *describing* and *explaining*. Questions can cover the following areas:

- *Content* e.g. characters; plot; setting; feelings/relationships; themes; ideas; arguments; facts/opinions
- *Composition* e.g. genre features; style; sentence structure; vocabulary and word choice; use of language including: similes, metaphors, alliteration, personification etc.
- *Technical* e.g. grammar, spelling (phonics) and punctuation in context; text layout/organisation

## CREATE SOMETHING GREAT

*Responding creatively to a text.*

May involve:

- Consolidating/using what's been learned during reading
- Solving a problem raised in text
- Researching/extending thinking on a subject or theme

Frequently includes:

- Drawing, designing, writing, planning, making, inventing, imagining, formulating, reconstructing, researching, composing, performing etc.
- *Creating a new text* as part of extended writing (can involve any subject area)

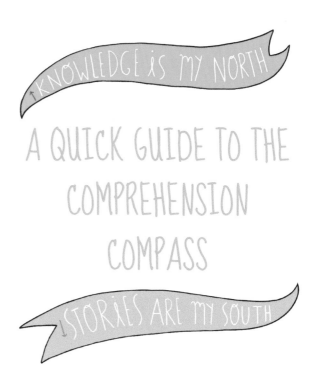

KNOWLEDGE IS MY NORTH

A QUICK GUIDE TO THE COMPREHENSION COMPASS

STORIES ARE MY SOUTH

## THE TASK MAP

The *'Task Map'* is the paper counterpart to the *Comprehension Compass*; it is used to display the tasks, activities and questions in a usable, visual format with an almost game-like appearance.

The format is entirely flexible; notice the headings come from the Compass segments. Depending on your age/ stage you may have more questions of a certain type than others. For example, when children are still in the earlier stages of learning to read, you may have two or three *Read & Understand* questions as they get to grips with finding answers in a text. When I was teaching further up the school, I tended to have at least two *Explore Some More* and two *Reflect and Respond* questions, as these tend to be more 'meaty'.

There is space to display eight tasks; if these are designed properly, there will actually be enough to cover all three days of your *Long Read* in class. Think of the *Task Map* as replacing old-fashioned comprehension exercises, where it would be 1-10 down the side of your jotter and ten often boring, generally literal, questions that had to be answered. Here, we obviously have fewer questions, but they will be high quality and involve higher order thinking. Groups will be able to discuss questions and work together, but ultimately, everyone in the group is responsible for writing down their own extended answer in their jotter.

One of the first improvements that you should notice when using *Task Maps* is that instead of a lack-lustre, one-line answer, children begin to write 'chunky paragraph' answers that are more sophisticated in content and structure.

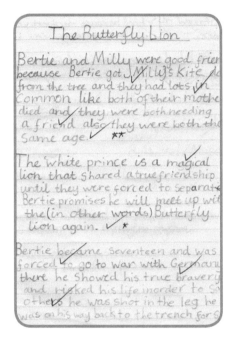

Read and Understand

Infer What's Not There

Read and Understand

Connect 4

GROUP CHAT

Reflective Reading

Text:

GO

Reflect and Respond

Create Something Great

Explore Some More

Explore Some More

### USING THE TASK MAP

The *Task Map* format can be used:

- On the whiteboard to display the choice of tasks and activities (for whole-class *Short Read* lessons)
- As a print out for reading groups with tasks and questions adjusted to enable differentiation (Long Read)
- As a blank document that children or reading groups complete with questions for their peers
- As an answer sheet to fill in responses to questions from the teacher or peers (although I do prefer jotters!)

### PERSONALISATION AND CHOICE

*Task Maps* have an element of choice built-in. The teacher can ask children to complete three, four, five, or more questions from the grid, individually, or as part of their group. Ask groups to tackle:

**Tic-Tac-Toe** or **Three in a Row**
**Connect Four**
**High Five**
**Pick Six**
**Select Seven**
or when they need a push:
**Full House**

Groups can decide themselves which questions they'd like to have a shot at. This works best if you have the groups sitting together, otherwise, shoulder-partners could decide which questions they will do.

### CREATE SOMETHING GREAT

Everyone always wants to do *Create Something Great* as it's usually an enjoyable, creative task. However, you need rules to deal with this, otherwise, everyone will be choosing that first and none of the 'real work' on comprehension will get done. There are a couple of ways to deal with this:

- Let everyone know they can **only** choose *Create Something Great* **after** they've completed the rest of their tasks.

- Keep *Create Something Great* a secret—do not even put it on the *Task Map* (replace it with an extra question). Tell the class that they will get to do the *most-exciting-top-secret-task* on Thursday or on your last *Long Read* session for the week.

### GROUP CHAT TASKS

The little 'GROUP CHAT' speech bubble can be placed on any part of the grid; it means that for this question you only have to discuss it  with your group. You don't need to write up your answer in your jotter—you don't even need to take notes! Naturally, this is another one children are drawn to as they think it's an easy option—so make sure that your questions are suitably challenging!

The other icon is the 'GO' arrow; use this if you want children to start with a particular question.  You could also make up your own icons e.g. a star or a tick for a question that you want everyone to attempt.

## Read and Understand

List all of the characters that appear in this film.

How did Paddington get his name?

## Infer What's Not There

Why do you think Paddington left Peru? How did he get to London?

Do you think there is a happy ending? What *clues* are there?

## Read and Understand

How does the mum feel about Paddington? (Give evidence for your answer.)

How does the dad feel about Paddington? (Give evidence for your answer.)

## Reflect and Respond

Would you like to go and see this film? Why/Why not?

Would you like to read the original books about Paddington? Why/Why not?

## Reflective Reading

**Text: Paddington Film Trailer**

http://youtu.be/7bZFr2IAOBo

*Text 2: Paddington TV Show
http://youtu.be/hdVPymvBCm8

## Connect 4

What do you know about London in your group? Make a quick mind map.

or

'*The film is always better than the book.*' Discuss.

GROUP CHAT

## Explore Some More

How does this trailer *persuade* us to go and see the film?

What *techniques* are used?

## Explore Some More

Close your eyes and listen to the soundtrack. What instruments do you hear?

Make a note of the words and feelings that come into your mind. Share your answers.

## Create Something Great

Imagine you find a bear in your street. Write the opening paragraphs of a story where you meet for the first time.

Watch the original Paddington TV show*: http://youtu.be/hdVPymvBCm8 What is the same/different? (MUST SEE!)

## TIME TO TEST OUT TASK MAPS

The best way to understand the *Task Map* system and how it works is to try it out for yourself. Either, have a go with colleagues in the comfort of the staffroom, or throw caution to the wind and try it out on your class first thing tomorrow morning!

The easiest *Task Maps* to start off with are:

***Paddington* Film Trailer** (see page 108)
**Breakfast Cereal** (opposite, page 110)

These ones can be used as whole-class *Task Maps*, so children can work in their mixed ability trios, or wherever they happen to be sitting. Print off enough *Task Maps*; one for each group—or simply display it on your (electronic) board. For the *Paddington* one, you'll need to find the trailer on YouTube. For the cereal one, you need to scour your cupboards or stop off at the supermarket to buy a box of breakfast cereal, one for each table. Try to get a different box for each group so you have a variety—it must be cereal that is aimed specifically at children.

There is no need to 'train' the children beforehand for this; you don't need to teach them about the *Comprehension Compass* and what the questions refer to. Give the groups the text and a *Task Map* and let them get on with it. You can drip-feed information to them, as required.

Gradually, through repeated use of the format, children will become familiar with the headings and the types of questions that fall under each one.

In the initial stages, all you're looking for is high motivation and engagement with the text and the questions—along with high quality discussion and answers.

In a short time, children will be experts in *Task Maps* and they'll even be able to have a go at creating their own *Task Map* grids, designing questions and activities for their peers—or younger classes—to complete.

## GET A PIZZA THE ACTION!

This a great activity to do towards the end of term.

- Give each group/table a cardboard pizza box (beg your local pizzeria establishment for a few boxes)
- Put 8 blank 'pizza slices' inside (just triangles of paper)
- Add a *different* text to each box

Groups have to read the text and come up with 8 questions using the Compass headings. They write the questions on the back of the pizza slices. (They can decorate/design/colour-in the front of their pizza slices if they wish.)

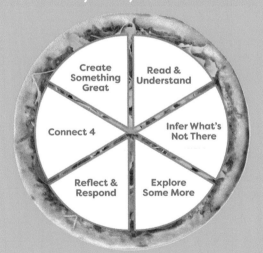

All groups swap boxes by delivering their Pizza Work Box to another table to complete.

The creators of each box are responsible for marking the answers!

Swap until each group has completed each pizza box!

## Read and Understand

What cereal do you have?

Who is the manufacturer and where do they make it?

**GO**

## Infer What's Not There

What ingredients are used in your cereal?

Do you think it sounds healthy? Why? Why not?

**Reflective Reading**

**Thinking About Advertising**

Text: **Breakfast Cereal Boxes**

## Reflect and Respond

What *techniques* are used on the box to *persuade* people to buy it or eat it?

Discuss and list as many as you can.

## Connect 4

Imagine and describe in detail what you would have for your 'Best Breakfast Ever'.

*Would this be a healthy choice?*

## Reflect and Respond

Do you think it is right that these cereals are advertised on children's television?

Why do companies do this?

## Explore Some More

Make a list of effective words and phrases that are used on the box.

## Explore Some More

Using the box, give:

- Two reasons why adults would buy this
- Two reasons why children would buy this

## Create Something Great

Create a new breakfast cereal. Come up with a name, logo, box and *slogan* in your group.

Draw a plate with your best breakfast ever on it.

## LONG READ WITH ABILITY GROUPS

If you're feeling a bit confused at the moment, that's entirely normal. You're probably trying to understand how to implement this and how this will actually work with ability groups, rather than as a whole-class. I will explain everything!

Firstly, I used the *Task Map* as a whole-class, mixed-ability lesson (Paddington and the cereal boxes) simply to demonstrate, in the easiest way, how the whole concept works.

I will now cover the most **Frequently Asked Questions** that teachers naturally have at this point; hopefully all will become clear.

### ISN'T THIS A SHORT READ ACTIVITY?

All of the *Task Map* examples in this book are suitable for *Short Read* purposes, as they use short, accessible texts that can be covered easily in one lesson. Can you use *Task Maps* on Mondays for *Short Read* sessions? Absolutely—I just don't recommend using them all the time. You want to keep your *Short Read* sessions fresh, fun and relevant. If you end up doing *Task Maps* Monday to Thursday, week after week, it can become boring very quickly; keep switching it up with a mixture of *TexTplorer* activities and *Task Maps*.

When the *Task Maps* are used in the *Long Read* sessions, **children are working in ability groups with differentiated texts**—which are naturally more complex than leaflets, trailers, adverts or poems.

### DO I HAVE TO MAKE A TASK MAP FOR EVERY READING GROUP?

Yes. If your groups are in genuine ability groups and really require different texts, then they will require different questions; ones that are appropriate for and **specific to** their text. My heart sinks when teachers ask me, 'Does that mean **I** need to read **all** of the books that they're reading?' Erm, yes, of course! How can you teach reading and discuss a text and its contents if you haven't read it?

Back to the original question. Yes, you will have to make a separate *Task Map* for each group that is reading a different text; in most cases, this will mean creating at least three Maps. But don't panic; this is easier and quicker than it sounds. You will have templates and ideas aplenty, and often, even though groups might be reading different books, they can still do some questions that are exactly the same or similar. Everyone can look at the 'author's use of language for effect' or do a 'VCOP Hunt' where they look for vocabulary, connectives, openers or punctuation in their text. Having some identical questions on the *Task Maps* will also enable you to 'pull the lesson together' at the end as you can discuss and compare what each group discovered about their text.

The more you get used to designing tasks with the Compass, the easier it becomes. In no time at all you'll be copying, pasting and tweaking your own questions, as you build up a valuable bank of resources.

There are several big pay-offs that mean, while a bit of time investment is required, especially at the beginning, the benefits of creating and using *Task Maps* are totally worth it—see the benefits box opposite.

## TASK MAPS = BIG BENEFITS

- Once you have created your Task Maps, that is *three full days of reading work* covered for each group. Preparation and planning—done!

- When working on the Task Maps the children will be working independently for the most part. They are working in groups/tables and will have a very high level of independence. This means you are free to go and work with children who require your support the most.

- You won't feel like you're 'chasing your tail' anymore in a lesson. You'll be able to circulate, help with problems, monitor and encourage, help extend thoughts and answers and give immediate feedback. You will even have time to stop and teach any important points that crop up along the way.

- The children themselves will enjoy this new way of working. They will adopt the new Long Read routine very quickly. They will be more motivated and enthusiastic about reading and completing comprehension tasks.

- You will notice an improvement in attitudes, and in progress. Discussions and written answers will be more complex, detailed and sophisticated.

- This new level of enthusiasm and leaning is what will keep you doing Task Maps— that and the fact that the children in your class will keep demanding them!

**Chris Joyce** @cjoyce21 · Mar 10
@anneglennie Boy in class after task map says "You've made us more clever with those TM's, I'd never be able to do those Qs before!" #fan#RR

&#8617;    &#8644; 1        &#9829; 1        •••

**Anne Glennie** @anneglennie · Mar 10
@cjoyce21 aww thanks Chris - that's wonderful news - that's my favourite kind of feedback! #reflectivereading #taskmaps :D

&#8617;    &#8644;        &#9829; 2    &#9636;    •••

**Chris Joyce**
@cjoyce21                                    ⚙  Following

@anneglennie just reassured me that it's worth the effort!! Seeing huge improvements and attitude to reading!! #taskmaps #reflectivereading

**Minnie MacLellan** @minniemacl · Jan 17
@anneglennie two years of using your #reflectivereading methodology and our reading attainment is soaring! #proudht

&#8617; 1    &#8644; 4        &#9829; 6

## WHERE DOES 'HEARING READING' FIT IN?

We'll cover 'hearing reading' in the next chapter: *Managing Reading in the Classroom.*

## COULD I USE THIS FOR HOMEWORK?

Yes, you could use the *Task Map* format for homework if you wanted, but I would advise against it. Sending it home will change the nature of the map from a collaborative task to an individual one. There is also a risk that children will see it as a 'chore' and you will lose the game-like quality. In terms of homework, I'd be much happier if children were actually reading instead of completing tasks. Today more than ever, reading is under threat from time, from technology and the availability of other forms of entertainment.

## DO I HAVE TO MAKE A TASK MAP FOR EVERY CHAPTER?

No, absolutely not—you will never be able to keep up with the reading—or the amount of work required. It depends on the book, how long chapters are and how quickly children are reading them. I would often have three chapters on one *Task Map* e.g. questions for *Charlotte's Web* chapters 3, 4 and 5 would be on the same sheet. But in this case, you'll need to put the chapter numbers beside each question, or simply number the questions from 1-8 in the order they should be attempted.

## HOW LONG SHOULD A LESSON BE?

How long is a piece of string? When planning for a language lesson I always allow myself around an hour. In reality, in the classroom, this might actually run over, especially if I'm going to do some direct teaching. As a whole-class lesson, my *Short Read* session on a Monday usually took us over the hour, but I felt it was justified for the high quality return I was getting from the children. But, there were of course times that the lesson was under an hour—especially as *Long Read* is happening on three days out of five. I used to have assembly before lunch every Thursday, so our *Long Read* session would generally be around 40 minutes, sometimes even less. You have to work with what you've got: your class, their needs, your groups, your timetable. Adapt everything until it fits, feels right and works for you and the children. You are the manager in your room; you're always in charge.

## AM I SUPPOSED TO BE DOING THIS IN PRIMARY 1 AND PRIMARY 2 (RECEPTION/Y1)?

As *Reflective Reading* is mainly about comprehension, it can be used fully from around Primary 3-4 (Y2-Y3 ).

Use in the Early Years will mainly be through the *Short Read* activities—using picture books and other texts to cover a wide range of literature and build up awareness and enjoyment of reading. It is desirable to use the *Comprehension Compass* when designing any activities/tasks/questions to go with these texts; higher order thinking skills are for everyone—including children further down the school.

The main literacy activities in any infant classroom should focus on teaching the alphabetic code and the skills of reading, writing and spelling to automaticity.

Comprehension will of course feature in this too, and where appropriate, teachers may wish to use a smaller version of the *Task Map*—with three boxes on a strip—to introduce questions related to their reading during phonics work and practice or in reading books given for reinforcement.

It might help to distinguish between 'learning to read' and 'reading to learn' — as the focus should be on the former in an Early Years classroom. I would be happy if teachers in P1/P2 (YR/Y1) were doing a quality, focused, relevant *Short Read* once a week, every week—along with all of the reading for pleasure that takes place naturally in this setting. Some able groups in P2/Y1 may cope with a full *Task Map* towards the end of the year.

## SHOULD MY LESS ABLE READERS BE DOING LONG READ ALONG WITH THE REST OF THE CLASS?

This is a brilliant question and one that strikes at the heart of the reading problem in many classrooms. Once children are in P3/P4 (Y2/Y3) onwards it is generally assumed that they have been taught to read/decode. And whilst that may be true, due to the ineffective methods and resources that are still employed in many schools, there are still a significant number of children who leave the infant stages unable to read. The problem is, no-one really continues to teach decoding further up the school, due to a lack of knowledge/resources/time and the pressure of other priorities.

However, it is imperative to find a solution to this issue and to eradicate poor practice. Who is at risk of reading failure in your school? What is being done about this?

Having Classroom Assistants or Pupil Support Assistants simply hearing groups of children read, and using a resource such as *Toe by Toe*, as the only reading input is woefully inadequate. Someone must have responsibility for actually teaching these children to read and spell—ideally that would be a teacher.

Giving children who are struggling beyond the early years the same books as children further down the school is unacceptable. Struggling readers should be using age-appropriate decodable reading books.

While it might seem kind to include children that are struggling with reading in *Long Read* lessons, by giving them an audio book or similar, this is absolutely not what they need. If a child can't read, write or spell adequately for their age/stage then it is essential that instruction in the basics continues. It may be that for three days a week, for as long as is necessary, the focus for these children is different to the rest of the class.

We have children for seven years in primary school, and while we may not succeed in making everyone love reading, we need to be sure that they are leaving us fully literate and capable of accessing their secondary curriculum with ease. It is our greatest priority. When it comes to basic skills, no-one should be left behind or forgotten.

I am well aware that time and resources mean that solutions are not always easy—but there are resources out there.

For primary literacy catch-up, if you are using a high quality phonics programme already, you should simply be able to use that, but depending on the resources and their styling, this may not always be practical/desirable.

I highly recommend this resource though, as it contains everything you need in one box for six struggling readers. There are nine workbooks for each child to work through and a teacher's guide for each one. Because the handbooks are so comprehensive, this catch-up intervention could be used by Classroom Assistants or PSAs. It is a solution in the box for every classroom where there are individuals struggling with reading.

***No Nonsense Phonics Skills Box Set***
by Debbie Hepplewhite
Raintree Publishing
ISBN: 9781474739665
www.raintree.co.uk

For secondary colleagues looking for suitable solutions, I recommend ***That Reading Thing.*** This is an age-appropriate literacy intervention that builds skills, knowledge and confidence in reading for teens and adults:
www.thatreadingthing.com

## MAKING YOUR OWN TASK MAPS

Over the next few pages there are additional *Task Maps* that can be used as stand-alone whole-class lessons, if you want to try them out before you begin making your own. That said, the best way to really see the potential of *Task Maps* in action is to tailor them to suit your class and whatever you're all reading.

When I do this part in training, everyone in the room watches the same trailer, then in our groups we come up with tasks and activities for each box on the *Task Map* template, then we share our ideas. It always amazes me that, although

we watched the same clip, the breadth and depth of questions is impressive. When you have completed your first grid full of tasks you should feel like you have something meaty, something juicy; something that will be challenging, engaging and enjoyable for your class.

Did someone say it's homework time? I'll just leave this here and I'll see you over in Chapter 6 when you're ready...

### MAKING TASK MAPS

Ideally, do this as a staff exercise; more brains are better than one for coming up with ideas and activities!

- Choose a text. A visual one is easiest, such as a film trailer, as this can be used at every stage e.g. for this exercise I use the trailer from the film 'The Fox and the Child' (U), or you could use one of the famous John Lewis Christmas adverts.

- Give each group/trio a blank Task Map.

- Watch the trailer/advert once without talking. Play it again; this time start coming up with ideas and questions in your group.

- Complete your Task Map as thoroughly as you can then share your wonderful ideas.

- Try your Maps out in class the next day. Have a debrief at your next staff meeting to see how everyone found it and decide on next steps for implementation.

# TASK MAPS: TOP TIPS

Don't worry about which questions go in which box—you will get the hang of it. Sometimes, you'll find that a question could actually go in multiple boxes, it doesn't matter; any good question goes on the grid! (If it is a research question though e.g. Now go and find out about foxes—that is a Create Something Great question and not Explore Some More. (Explore Some More is looking at an aspect of the text itself in more detail.)

Don't be afraid to put a double-whammy or a triple-whammy question in one box—you can put an easier task in there sandwiched by more demanding ones.

All boxes should have an element of challenge. Be prepared to tweak questions to ensure they have plenty of work to do: e.g. *What seasons are shown in the film?* would be better as: *How does the director show the passing of each season?* Always read your question back—if it can be answered with one word, or a 'yes' or 'no'—it needs tweaking.

Ramp up the rewards for difficult tasks. My original idea was that the Task Map/Comprehension Compass would be like Trivial Pursuit: every group would have to answer a question of every type to get their full 'cheese', or 'wheel' if you know what I mean? You could award points and/or prizes for groups that get a 'Full House'.

All questions should be discussed as group—but written down in a full answer in a jotter by each individual.

The format is flexible—but do include at least one of each question type. Ensure your map is balanced and has a good mix of tasks—so that children can't avoid hard work—even if they want to.

Don't feel that every chapter has to have its own Task Map—chapters can be combined on one sheet.

If you want to try Task Maps in P1/P2 (YR/Y1) a 'strip of three' grid can be used as a starting point.

Don't panic about 'reading' visual texts such as trailers, films or adverts. It's really just the same as any other text; the only other things you may wish to consider are: camera angles and the soundtrack/sound effects e.g. Why did the director use a close-up here? What effect does it have? How does the soundtrack make you feel? Why is the soundtrack effective? etc.

The three Cs are also useful: *Character, Colour, Camera* and the three Ss: *Setting, Sound, Story* as starting points for questions based around a visual or moving image text.

# Question Prompts for Moving Image Texts

## THE THREE Cs

### CAMERA
What can be seen in the frame & why?
What camera movement is happening & why?
What height or angle is the camera at & why?
What might be anything excluded from the frame?
If the camera is the narrator, what is it saying?
How long is the shot?
What was the previous/next shot & why?

### CHARACTER
What do we know (imagine) about this character?
What do the clothes tell us?
Where do they live?
What do they eat?
What are their qualities? (emotional, skills, behaviour)
What is their motivation/aim/desire?
What are their obstacles to achieving their goal?

### COLOUR
What does this colour mean?
Are any characters associated with a particular colour?
Is there a tone/colour scheme to the film?
Are the colours mostly light/dark?
Can colours change meaning?
How is light used in the film?

## THE THREE Ss

### SETTING
What is the setting in terms of time(year/date/morning/evening)?
What is the setting in terms of place?
What is the setting in terms of genre?
How does the soundtrack support the setting?
How would the film be different if it was set in an alternative setting?
Is the set constructed or real? How do you know?
Is this the natural/comfortable setting for the characters?

### SOUND
What does the sound track tell us?
How is music used?
What is the emotional content of the music?
Find out what "diegetic" means.
Identify diegetic sounds in the film.
What sounds are heard "off screen" or out of shot?

### STORY
Discuss the story.
Does the story have a beginning, middle and end?
Is the story clear? If not how could the film makers make it clear?
How do all of the above contribute to the telling of the story?

www.floodfilm.com/literacy/3cs-and-3ss/
Reproduced with kind permission of Tim Flood of Flood Films

## Read and Understand

Choose 4 tricky/interesting words from the text. Discuss and note their meanings:

1. protagonist
2.
3.
4.

## Reflect and Respond

*'World Book Day is just a waste of time and money'.*

Discuss in your group, giving reasons for your answer.

## Explore Some More

Copy this grid into your jotter. Note all the reasons 'For' and 'Against' WBD that are mentioned in the articles.

| For WBD | Against WBD |
| --- | --- |
| | |

## Infer What's Not There

1. Make a list of all the people or businesses that benefit from WBD in some way.

2. Discuss and Decide:
Who gets the most benefit from WBD? Who gets the least?

## Reflective Reading

**Text: World Book Day**
**(Article and Blog—Read BOTH texts)**

 3 MUST DO + choose 1 GROUP CHAT
+ 1 other

## Explore Some More

Notice how the paragraphs are laid out in the articles. Now look at a fiction book and compare the layout.

How does the layout differ?

## Reflect and Respond

How does Daddacool get his children to read? Should parents do this? Why?

What is in the bag on Daddacool's desk?
(*Infer*)

## Connect 4

For you, what is the best thing about World Book Day?

OR

*Reading offers a lifetime of pleasure.'*
Do you agree? Why? Why not?

## Create Something Great

Imagine you are a blogger. Write a 100 words about your personal views on WBD. Include:

Blog Name and Logo
Headline
An illustration by you
Imaginary web address

# DADDACOOL

## "BRITAIN'S PREMIER PARENT BLOGGER" SUNDAY TIMES

# IT'S TIME TO RECLAIM WORLD BOOK DAY

Sitting next to me on my desk is a multi-coloured fluffy monstrosity. It's in a bag fortunately, for if it wasn't I fear my both my sight and sanity. It is Fifi's reward for reading an entire chapter book over half term. We love reading and try to encourage our kids to grow their love of it by bribery.

And yet as *World Book Day* approaches, my Twitter timeline is full of retailers selling Disney Princess costumes, Darth Vader suits and comic book superhero costumes for the inevitable "school dressing up day" that seems to be what *World Book Day* has become. To save parents the time, hassle and panic, why not drop the whole dressing up thing and spend the day more notably focused on fostering a genuine love of reading?

Currently, number one child is confused as how to dress up like his favourite book character as he's enjoying the *Middle School* books. The main protagonist is Rafe Khatchadorian, a child who dresses like a child would. How do you dress up so you can be identified as that character? You can't; you pick someone who is recognisable from a book you've either read and didn't go on much or from a movie you've seen based on a book you might have read.

It's a complete waste of time and a distraction from what is a great opportunity for kids to spend time with a good book in an environment where there aren't the tech distractions that you have at home.

Come on! Let's reclaim *World Book Day* from the fancy dress retailers!!!

SHARE THIS:

*IT'S TIME TO RECLAIM WORLD BOOK DAY* by DADDACOOL
Text adapted from http://www.daddacool.co.uk/2017/02/time-reclaim-world-book-day.html
Reproduced with permission of the author, Alex Walsh

At the Heart of Publishing since 1858

# World Book Day: quarter of children would not own a book without it

Research revealed on World Book Day (WBD) suggests that a quarter of eight to 11-year-olds would not own a book without the initiative.

The National Literary Trust's survey of more than 9,000 pupils has shown that nine out of 10 (89.5%) were aware of the event and that almost 60% were inspired to read more because of it. One in four children (25.2%) said that the first book they had ever bought was with the WBD token issued last year.

*Pupils from Saint Rose of Lima School in Glasgow celebrate World Book Day*

Kirsten Grant, WBD director, said: "We're extremely proud of how deep the impact of World Book Day continues to be in the lives of children and young people all over the UK, particularly in light of the recent news that one in ten people don't own a single book.

Evidence suggests that there is a lost generation of readers amongst today's adults, but we truly hope that, through giving children and young people greater access to books, World Book Day is ensuring that the next generation carry a love of reading with them on into adulthood. We want to empower children to make choices about what they want to read, and inspire them to be regular visitors to their local bookshop and library. Reading can offer a lifetime of pleasure."

Tokens can be exchanged for one of 10 specially-published £1 WBD books. David Walliams' offering, *Blob*, landed straight in the UK Official Top 50 number one spot, it was revealed this week.

**World Book Day: quarter of children would not own a book without it**
Published March 1, 2017 by Heloise Wood
Text adapted from http://www.thebookseller.com/news/one-four-childrens-first-book-bought-wbd-token-499621
Reproduced with permission of *The Bookseller*

# For my Grandmother Knitting

There is no need they say
but the needles still move
their rhythms in the working of your hands
as easily
as if your hands
were once again those sure and skilful hands
of the fisher-girl.

You are old now
and your grasp of things is not so good
but master of your moments then
deft and swift
you slit the still-ticking quick silver fish.
Hard work it was too
of necessity.

But now they say there is no need
as the needles move
in the working of your hands
once the hands of the bride
with the hand-span waist
once the hands of the miner's wife
who scrubbed his back
in a tin bath by the coal fire
once the hands of the mother
of six who made do and mended
scraped and slaved slapped sometimes
when necessary.

But now they say there is no need
the kids they say grandma
have too much already
more than they can wear
too many scarves and cardigans –
gran you do too much
there's no necessity....

At your window you wave
them goodbye Sunday.
With your painful hands
big on shrunken wrists.
Swollen-jointed. Red. Arthritic. Old.
But the needles still move
their rhythms in the working of your hands
easily
as if your hands remembered
of their own accord the pattern
as if your hands had forgotten
how to stop.

## Liz Lochhead

*For my Grandmother Knitting* by Liz Lochhead
from *A Choosing: Selected Poems* (Polygon 2011)
Reproduced with permission of Birlinn through PLSclear

## Reflect and Respond

Poetry is written to be read aloud. Take turns reading this line aloud. Can you explain why this line is effective?

*'you slit the still-ticking quick silver fish'*

What does this line mean?

## Connect 4

Can you knit? Is it an important skill today? Discuss.

GROUP CHAT

Do you visit any older relatives or grandparents? Do you know what job they used to do?

## Create Something Great

Now write your own poem. Choose a person you know well and write a descriptive poem about them. You could focus on their hands and what they do.

Or choose a favourite meal and write about who makes it, how they do it and how it makes you feel. Share your work.

## Infer What's Not There

Who comes to visit the grandmother on Sunday?

What do they tell her? Why?

## Reflective Reading

**Text: For My Grandmother Knitting by Liz Lochhead**

Listen to the teacher read the poem *Grandpa's Soup* by Jackie Kay, before you begin.

## Explore Some More

Can you spot any special techniques that the poet uses? Give examples and try to explain why they are effective.

*(Clues: repetition, punctuation, alliteration, assonance)*

## Read and Understand

What is the poem about? Is it really about knitting? Or something else? Explain your answer.

What facts do we learn about the Grandmother and her life? Make a list.

## Reflect and Respond

How does the poem make you feel?

Did you enjoy it? Why? Why not?

Do you prefer *For My Grandmother Knitting* or *Grandpa's Soup?*

## Explore Some More

Make a list of all of the adjectives used in the poem that describe the Grandmother.

Is it a positive or negative list? Explain your answer.

# Managing Reading in the Classroom

# CHAPTER 6
# Managing Reading in the Classroom

In this chapter we'll take a look at how to manage reading on a daily basis, at a practical level. I'll also pull together any issues that haven't been addressed so far.

## READING PRACTICE

Are your children getting enough reading practice? To become the type of reader we would like every member of our class to be—confident, fluent, capable—it is going to take a lot of practice. It would be interesting to audit the actual amount of time your class spend engaged in the act of reading every day/week/month.

The cumulative effect of daily reading at school (and at home) is huge. Knowledge, vocabulary, skill and stamina are building away in the background. Anyone not participating in this is at a serious disadvantage. Protecting and prioritising time for reading every day is crucial. Examine your ERIC time—does it happen every day, no matter what? Is it valued? How do you know? How do the children know? Are reading choices discussed, monitored, encouraged? Are the reading materials on offer sufficiently motivating and enticing? Is everyone *really* reading? Are they so engrossed with their book that it's hard to get their attention back? That's what you're after: flow.

During English (Language) lessons what and how much are children reading? Consider, Billy, for a moment. He doesn't

have any books at home. In fact, if you ask him, he'll tell you that the only book in his house is the Argos catalogue. It's pretty much going to be up to his teachers to introduce Billy to the power and magic of words and books.

Now consider what reading material we are offering Billy in the earliest stages of his journey to being a reader. Is his reading book over 20 years old? Is it attractive? Is it appropriate? Is he reading about the same family from the same reading scheme for three years? Will this widen his horizons?

The only book in Billy's house is the Argos catalogue.

We can change our practice. We can change our pedagogy. But if the actual books on offer are past their sell-by-date and offer little in the way of relevance/ interest/imagination, then we still have a problem.

I regularly meet teachers who are using the **same** books to teach reading to their class **that they had when they were at school**.

Reading books and reading schemes are expensive, but so are many things schools spend money on. If reading is a priority in your school then the books and materials you use to teach reading are a priority too; they are the tools for the job.

## HEARING READING

Thinking about Billy again. What does he actually *do* with his reading book? Does he sit with his group and read it out loud to the teacher or a classroom assistant when it's his turn? Is the scene in the photo below from 1952 a blast from the past? Or is it happening in a school near you? This is **hearing reading**. And if you do nothing else after reading this book, please, stamp-out hearing reading. It is a waste of time.

Have a look at the picture. Can you spot the children that: have already switched off because they've had their turn; are

following with their finger, desperately trying to work out which bit they're going to be asked to read next; the girls that are getting nervous because it's nearly their turn? And what about the teacher—what is she thinking about? GIN! (Please don't write in, I'm only joking...) But if we're honest, we've all been there; hearing the reading, but not listening.

Instead of 'hearing' reading, think about 'seeing' reading in action. Here are the different types of reading that you might see in a classroom:

- **Individual Silent Reading** (for fun: ERIC etc. and for learning)
- **Individual Reading Aloud** (skills practice)
- **Paired Reading**
- **Group Reading** (*Short Read*: Follow the Reader)
- **Buddy Reading/Peer Mentoring** (mixed age/stage)
- **Whole-Class/Choral Reading**
- **Teacher and Child: One to One** (coaching/dialogue)
- **Teacher Reading to Class** (for learning, for fun, forever…

## INDIVIDUAL READING ALOUD

This could also be called *'Reading Aloud Alone'* and is a strategy I was introduced to fairly recently. Essentially, this involves the child reading to themselves, but rather than doing this silently, or internally, they read out loud instead, using a soft voice. This is particularly effective when children are learning to read because it gives them extra practice at decoding and blending. It's important because as children read aloud, they are matching, or mapping, their spoken words with the written text; translating the written word back into the spoken word. This practice helps not only that connection, but fluency, accuracy and speed. As mentioned already, when children read silently they have a tendency to skip words, but if they are reading aloud, even without an audience, they have to give it a go.

Remember too that when children are learning to read, when they read a text for the first time, all of their brain power is devoted to decoding it, to getting the words off the page. There will be no brain power or bandwidth left for actually understanding the text or deciding what will happen next. At this stage we need to give children multiple opportunities to read: to read for decoding, then to read again to understand and consider what's actually going on.

You've probably experienced something similar, if you've read a bible passage out in church or at a school assembly. Even as adults in this scenario, we are focussed on reading well, clearly, turning the page, using an appropriate pace, tone and emphasis. As we read in these circumstances, we are not actually paying attention to understanding the content— we are only dealing with the job at hand.

## PAIRED READING

If you're still 'hearing reading' I recommend that you give *Paired Reading* a try. This is easy-peasy to implement and it will save you so much time.

At the start of my *Long Read* session, especially if we're using chapter books/ novels, I allow around ten minutes of silent reading, so that children can read the chapter or pages they're going to have questions on that day.

Originally, when I used to use *Literature Circles*, this reading would be done at home, as part of homework. But not everyone would do it, and those that did were finding it a chore and complaining that this took away their time for reading for pleasure. I also felt that as a teacher, I wasn't really teaching anything about reading, I was simply 'facilitating' a book discussion. I then decided to allow time in class for this reading instead.

Once children have spent ten minutes reading the day's chapter, I would then get them to read in pairs for around five minutes or so. This is children in the same ability group, studying the same book. They take turns reading out loud, and then they coach each other and give feedback, based on FASE:

F:    FLUENCY
A:    ACCURACY
S:    SPEED
E:    EXPRESSION*

They can then fill in and 'traffic light' their *Reading Record Sheet* in their jotter. (see opposite)

* ***Expression*** is a 'nice to have', but note that not everyone will achieve this.

# My Reading Record

Name [ ]   Class [ ]

Book [ ]   Author [ ]

**Reflective Reading**

| Date | Pages | Traffic Light | Comment: How is your FASE?<br>Fluency: Accuracy, Speed and Expression | Signed |
|------|-------|---------------|-----------------------------------------------------------------------|--------|
| | | | | |
| | | | | |
| | | | | |
| | | | | |
| | | | | |
| | | | | |
| | | | | |
| | | | | |
| | | | | |
| | | | | |
| | | | | |
| | | | | |
| | | | | |
| | | | | |
| | | | | |
| | | | | |

My Reading Record

### BUDDY READING/PEER MENTORING

Peer mentoring, or 'Buddy Reading', as it's sometimes known, is a lovely strategy and can be used to great effect to bolster the confidence and reading enjoyment of everyone involved. Most commonly, this is done in mixed stages—so you might have the P7s (Y6s) reading to/with the P1s (YR).

If you haven't tried it, it is worth giving it a go. However, there are some things to think about. Buddy reading in this way is definitely a 'one-hit-wonder'; it should not be used for the whole year, but for a term at the very most. The reason for this is that although the benefits may continue for the younger children, the benefits for the older children have already been realised—they would now be better spending time on pushing ahead with their own reading progress, building stamina and skills in reading more sophisticated and complex texts.

It's also worth noting that the best results are to be had when there isn't such a huge gap between the age/stage. For example, having P6 (Y5) work with P3 (Y2) or P4 (Y3) has been shown to have more impact.

### TEACHER AND CHILD: ONE TO ONE

For those of you that are panicking, don't worry, I do still think it's important for teachers to listen to children reading; I just don't think we need to attempt to listen to more than one child at a time. In the 'hearing reading' scenario, while we listen to one child reading, the others are not benefitting in any way—they'd be better off doing something more productive with their time than simply waiting for their turn.

One of the real advantages of using *Task Maps* is that, once they have the hang of it, children will be working away in their groups independently. This allows me to go where I am needed, to listen to children read as required and to focus on my priorities. Reading fluency is only one aspect of reading, it shouldn't take up the bulk of my lesson. I might listen to Billy read every day, if that's what he needs. But I might also be teaching him, working with him feedback or assessing him. I might only listen to Natalie read once every three weeks, to check-in—and spend that time discussing questions and answers with her group instead.

### TEACHER READING TO THE CLASS

We've covered this already in previous chapters, but it's worth repeating.

Carve out time to read to your class every day; no matter what else comes your way. Justify it until the cows come home; defend it with your dying breath. Never underestimate the power and joy of reading to your class and the lasting impact it can have on children, not just today, but for the rest of their lives.

Reading Buddies

## WHOLE-CLASS/CHORAL READING

*Choral Reading* is a great reading strategy to use in the classroom: it's an enjoyable activity that practises reading aloud whilst ensuring that everyone is involved and engaged at all times. It also improves everyone's **FASE** (*Fluency, Accuracy, Speed* and *Expression*)!

Poems, songs, raps and short rhyming stories are all ideal texts to try out with choral reading. To keep everyone in time, I usually tap out a 4/4 beat on the table with a chopstick or pen. (Count everyone in on 4, and keep the same rhythm e.g 1, 2, 3, 4; 1, 2, 3, 4.)

The next time you're on YouTube—search for 'choral reading' to see examples of classes (with perfect clothes, movements and diction—it's actually a bit scary!) performing and competing while reading their favourite texts aloud. Show your class and tell them this is what you're looking for!

## LOVE YOUR LIBRARY

I'm aware that some schools don't have a library and this is generally not through choice. (Unless you had one and turned it into an ICT room instead—what *were* you thinking?)

Resourcing issues aside, if you don't have a library, you need one. If we want children to read, they need access to a wide range of books and reading materials aka *a library*.

If you don't have a spare room, is there a corridor, a cupboard or a corner that you could convert? Could you get creative with shelving (see 'gutter book shelves'

on *Pinterest*) and seating? Could you involve parents, the community and local businesses by inviting them to donate a new book with a dedication inside? Beg. Borrow. Steal. (*OK,* forget that last one.) Put the *fun* into *fun*raising and get everyone on board with building a home for books in your school.

Need inspiration? Visit this wonderful site to drool over their design gallery:

**www.bookspaceforschools.co.uk**

Your library is an enterprise waiting to happen:

- Is it well-used, welcoming and busy?
- Does it open before and after school?
- Is it stocked with a wide range of attractive materials, including newspapers and magazine subscriptions?
- Are new titles publicised at assembly?
- Are there exciting displays of books, reviews, characters or story-inspired art?
- Do you have a scheduled Story Time at lunch-time each day, run by children or parents? Will it be outside instead if the weather's good?
- Do children check the books in and out? Can they suggest titles for purchase?
- Do you have a Book Group or a Writing Club?

Note:

A Book Group for children is the same as for adults—except there is no wine involved!

## READING FOR PLEASURE

In Chapter 1, we looked at the importance of reading for pleasure, but how do we ensure that it becomes a daily habit and action at school and at home, rather than a worn-out mantra?

I propose that you relaunch reading, give it a face-lift and a catchy new slogan! Announce it at assembly as a whole-school initiative and give it a high profile. I suggest: *5, 4, 3, 2, 1, THUNDERBOOKS* or *High Five!* but I'm sure you could come up with something better.

It's like your 5-a-day for fruit and veg, but even more exciting because it comes with a choice of not one, but three, crowd-rowsing theme tunes!

You can use:

- *5, 4, 3, 2, 1 by Manfred Mann*
- *The Thunderbirds opening titles and theme tune*
- *The Hawaii Five-O theme tune*

Here I'm suggesting that children, parents and teachers all share the reading responsibility. We need to recognise that while we may not always read in every way, every day—these are all desirable behaviours; we should be conscious of them and encourage them.

The *5, 4, 3, 2, 1*, of reading then is:

- **5:** Children read at ERIC time
- **4:** Children read their reading book (the one they're using for *Long Read*)
- **3:** The teacher reads to the class
- **2:** Someone at home reads to child/ children
- **1:** Child chooses to read at home

For number 2: someone reading to the child at home, this can be a parent, grandparent, a brother or sister. It can even be a story CD or an audio book in the car. Everyone is busy—but we need to find ways of fitting reading in.

Similarly, for Number 1 and children reading at home—anything goes. This can be an ERIC book, a school book, a personal book/comic/magazine etc.

The 5-a-day reading concept can be as simple or as elaborate as you like. Children can share their '5-a-day' books from the previous week—and they could get a high five and a certificate or a sticker—or even better: a bookmark.

My favourite reading quote of all time is this one by Oscar Wilde, for me it sums up the influence books and reading can have, not just on our thoughts, but on who we are, as people.

> "It is what you read when you don't have to that determines what you will be when you can't help it."
>
> OSCAR WILDE

**5** I read at ERIC time today! Yay!

**4** I read my reading book in class!

My teacher read to the class today. **3**

**2** Someone read to me at home.

I read something at home. **1**

## ENGAGING PARENTS WITH READING AT HOME

If we want parents to share the responsibility for reading, then we have to engage with them and communicate our expectations. The best way to do this is at school, by combining a 'parent pop-in' with a short meeting. Offer two 'strands': a meeting that explains how we teach reading and the resources and methods we use, for parents of children in infants, and one for parents of P4-P7 (Y3-Y6) children.

Teach parents how to support their children with reading instruction by explaining how systematic synthetic phonics works; show them the alphabetic code and how letters and sounds are linked. Teach them the same simple hand movements that are used in class: finger tracking under letters, whilst saying the sounds, then blending to make a word. Explain how to orally segment words for spelling, and how to count or tally the sounds, before writing them down.

These strategies are relevant and helpful; they relate to the knowledge of the letter/sound correspondences being taught and to the actual skills of reading and spelling.

Avoid other strategies that are of little practical value, such as *'pause, prompt, praise'* or ones that resort to guessing, such as: **look at the picture** (and guess), **look at the first letter** (and guess the rest), **read on** (and guess what might fit), **look at the last letter** (which is of little use to anyone...). Also abandon breaking a word into syllables; when learning to read, the **phoneme** (sound) is the only unit of sound that is necessary.

Combine these meetings with a short classroom visit where their children can show them their work and they can perhaps see part of a lesson in action. If we want support from parents we need to show them what that looks like in reality.

In all cases, emphasise the importance of reading and talking to/with their children; reading for pleasure and its benefits; general knowledge and vocabulary and its impact on comprehension. Share the research with them explaining how good habits in these areas can make an enormous and lasting difference to their child's education.

Be aware that it may also be increasingly necessary to provide guidelines to parents about screen time, sleep and so on, as they have an impact on children's ability to perform at school.

A sample leaflet for parents/carers is provided over the next couple of pages.

You may wish to use this as a template to design your own school information.

# READ TO SUCCEED

## How to Help with Reading at Home

- Put a couple of 'Book Boxes' or 'Book Baskets' around the house with some interesting reading material inside—you could even put one in the 'Reading Room' aka the bathroom!

- Set a timer for 10 or 15 minutes and get everyone to read together in the same room; after dinner works well or before bed is ideal too.

- Have a 'Switch-Off' Sunday—go analogue for the afternoon. No screens allowed—just reading and/or family games.

- Tempt everyone to the table with a 'Booky Breakfast' have a different breakfast like pancakes and fruit—with a side order of books.

**Children who read, succeed. End of story.**

### Did you know?

Children whose parents regularly read aloud with them in the first year of primary school performed substantially better in reading at age 15 than children whose parents rarely, if ever, read to them.

**OECD
What Can Parents Do**

## HEALTHY HABITS

When it comes to reading materials anything goes. Books, ebooks, audio books, newspapers, free supermarket magazines, comics, leaflets, recipes and so on. If you can, visit your local library —there will be something to interest even your most reluctant readers there, including books on their favourite TV characters or games.

The pace of life today is more hectic than ever, but building in book time can be a great way to relax and unwind. Find a reading habit that you can fit into daily or weekly life...

Research to signpost and share:

- Parents and the home environment are essential to the early teaching of reading and fostering a love of reading; children are more likely to continue to be readers in homes where books and reading are valued (Clark and Rumbold, 2006).

- Reading for pleasure is strongly influenced by relationships between teachers and children, and children and families (Cremin et al, 2009).

- Children whose parents regularly read aloud with them in the first year of primary school performed substantially better in reading at age 15 than children whose parents rarely, if ever, read to them (*What Can Parents Do to Help Their Children Succeed in School*, OECD).

### RECOMMENDED WEBSITES FOR PARENTS/CARERS

The following websites about reading instruction are useful, for parents and carers in particular.

### *Teaching Children to Read and Write*

**www.tcrw.co.uk**

TCRW stands for *Teaching Children to Read and Write*. This comprehensive resource was put together by Sue Lloyd of **Jolly Phonics** fame. It's ideal for parents as it is presented through a series of very clear, easily-digested videos, all presented by Sue Lloyd herself.

### *Help Your Child to Read and Write*

**www.udemy.com/help-your-child-to-read-and-write/**

This is actually a free, online, hour-long course by John Walker of **Sounds Write**. It is aimed at parents or carers who want to give their children aged 4 to 6 a good start in learning to read and spell. (It is not really designed for teachers or for helping older children who have reading difficulties.)

If you can't get parents to commit to a meeting in school, this could be an ideal solution as it can be viewed on mobile phones, tablets and smart TVs.

### YOUR READING WEEK

On page 138 there are some sample weekly timetables, to illustrate what your full week might look like in terms of English/Language lessons. These show the differences between stages and highlight some issues that may arise. Many of the examples are composite classes, as these are common where I was teaching in the Western Isles.

### WHOLE-CLASS NOVELS

You will notice that when one of our class projects was *Charlie and the Chocolate Factory,* we read the novel as a whole class, or rather, we listened to the audio book. Is this allowed? Yes, of course: *'as I read, listen or watch'* is part of our new definition of reading. Could I do this all the time? Definitely not. I would say that you could probably get away with a whole-class novel (as your reading book/*Long Read* text) once or twice a year at the most; certainly for no longer than four weeks out of a full session.

## Did you know?

**Research shows that children are more likely to continue to be readers in homes where books and reading are valued**

## BOOKS FOR BEDTIME

At school, your child will practise their reading skills through lots of different activities. You can help at home by reading to your child/children too.

A bedtime story is an ideal way to end the day. Bath, bed, book—is a brilliant routine when you can manage it.

Even when your child can read, it's still worthwhile to read something together that is too hard for them to read on their own.

Don't have time for a chapter a night? Share a favourite picture book, a poem, some jokes or even a comic—or an article from a magazine; something is better than nothing.

On nights when life is just too busy, fit reading in by using a story CD or an audio book, which are good options for bedtime—or for when you're out and about in the car.

## HOW TO HELP WITH READING HOMEWORK

The good news is that you only need to know one trick when your child is learning to read: it's all about the *sounds* we say when we see the letters: /k/ /a/ /t/.

If your child is stuck on a word, ask them to '*sound it out*'. Put your finger under each letter as they say the sounds—then *blend those sounds together* to make a word.

Guessing should not be used. All the clues you need are on the page—the letters!

Your child's school will be able to give you further advice about how you can help.

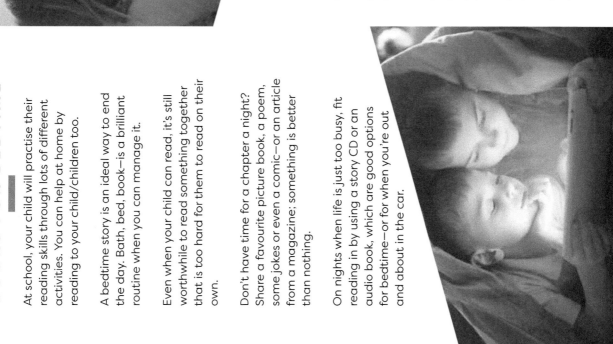

## READING FOR PLEASURE

As teachers, parents and carers we must do whatever we can to encourage our children to read for pleasure: as a choice, as a hobby, and as a habit.

Children who regularly read for fun improve their vocabulary, their spelling and writing—it can even have a positive impact on maths!

The research is clear: children who read for pleasure succeed, at primary school and beyond. Not only that, but reading is great for relaxation and is an ideal way to give children a break from screen time and computer games.

Reading for fun can increase your child's self-confidence in reading, it also helps them understand different cultures, lives, and points of view—it can even make them smarter!

This is because we must be conscious of providing appropriate texts, pace and challenge for everyone; we must cater for all of the needs in the class, whether that means stretching or supporting.

However, I do like to imagine a day when, if we teach all of our children to read properly, from the beginning of Primary 1/Reception, that by Primary 4/Year 3 at the very latest, then whole-class novels could make a comeback, because, well, everyone could read them. Imagine the quality of work that would be possible, the depth of discussion—the teaching and learning—if everyone could share the reading experience and the motivating context.

It shouldn't be so difficult to envisage. After all, once at secondary school, all children use the *same texts* for reading and study; it is simply expected that they can read them. This should perhaps give us cause for reflection again on the nature and use of differentiation in primary schools. Does it create more problems than it solves? And do we *really* need all of these reading groups?

## READING INTO WRITING

In the sample timetables, you will notice that the extended writing lesson on the Friday is almost always linked to the *Short Read* lesson from the start of the week. You don't have to do this, but your writing results will be so much better when you do. Because the *Short Read* lesson involves the whole class, it is the ideal forum to prepare for writing at the end of the week. This might be because you will be studying a text or extract that involves one or more of the following:

- ***relevant content***

Often we ask children to write about things they know very little about. '*Write an argument 'for' or against' zoos*', for example. Do they know what the issues are that affect the animals? Are they aware of both sides of the argument: the advantages of keeping animals in captivity, the disadvantages? Do they even have an opinion at the moment? Your *Short Read* can cover all of these, including background information, content and vocabulary, so that children will already have some insight and something to say come Friday.

- ***text type/genre features***

If I want my class to write a particular type of text, it makes sense for us to study the text type and its features. Rather than try to do this before our extended writing, it 'kills two birds with one stone' if we explore a model text as part of *Short Read*. If we're going to be writing a newspaper report, a letter, a detailed setting description on Friday? Guess what we'll be looking at on Monday—and I'll be sure to draw attention to and teach about any relevant features.

- ***writer's craft tools and techniques***

Sometimes, I might choose a *Short Read* text because it illustrates a particular teaching point. This could be an aspect of creative writing, such as figurative language e.g similes/metaphors, personification that I want to teach or revise. Or it could be that, through formative assessment, I've identified a particular development need. For example, if I'm noticing that punctuation of direct speech keeps cropping up as an issue in written work, then the following week I might want to choose a text that will help me show my class how to do it

# Overview: My Reading Week: Sample Timetables

| CLASS/PROJECT DAY/Lesson | P1-P2/P3 (YR-Y1/Y2) THE SEASIDE | Primary 4/5 (Year3/4) ROALD DAHL | Primary 3/4/5 (Year2/3/4) CHARLIE & THE CHOC. FACTORY | Primary 6/7 (Year 5/6) WW2 | Primary 7 (Year 6) SOLAR SYSTEM |
|---|---|---|---|---|---|
| MONDAY Short Read | The Snorgh and the Sailor Phonic Work & Practice* (reading, writing, spelling) | Roald Dahl biography, YouTube poems, extracts, Picture It: Trunchbull | Recipes, how choc is made, Dahl biography, news article on children & YouTube | BBC Drama 'Anne Frank', WW2 poetry, non-fiction etc. | Integrate It: ISS, Alien Postcard Poems, various non-fiction etc. |
| TUESDAY Long Read | Phonic Work & Practice* (reading, writing, spelling) | G1: The BFG G2: The Twits G3: Dahl Poems | Class Novel C&C Factory Audio Book | G1: Anne Frank G2: Anne Frank G3: Reading Intervention | All groups on different reading scheme books |
| WEDNESDAY Long Read | Phonic Work & Practice* (reading, writing, spelling) | G1: The BFG G2: The Twits G3: Dahl Poems | Class Novel C&C Factory Audio Book | G1: Anne Frank G2: Anne Frank G3: Reading Intervention | All groups on different reading scheme books |
| THURSDAY Long Read | Phonic Work & Practice* (reading, writing, spelling) | G1: The BFG G2: The Twits G3: Dahl Poems | Class Novel C&C Factory Audio Book | G1: Anne Frank G2: Anne Frank G3: Reading Intervention | All groups on different reading scheme books |
| FRIDAY Extended Writing | Write your own Snorgh adventure or write new rules for Snorghs | Create your own character & write a Dahl-style description | Various text types, linked to Short Read e.g. recipe, biography etc. | Various text types, linked to Short Read e.g. poems, instructions, diary etc. | Various texts e.g. write letter to parents before going to space, job application Space Academy |

*Phonic work and practice should take place on 4 days out of 5 and include word, sentence and text level work as well as reading, writing and spelling.

properly e.g. a conversation from the BFG between Sophie and the giant. This allows me to draw attention to it in context and explain it in a meaningful way. In addition to this, it is also good practice to do some direct teaching and provide examples for the children to work through and practise on—this is one of the real advantages of a whole-class lesson.

How would this work in reality? I might say, 'Ok everyone, today, when you're finished your *Blankety Blank/Picture It/ Task Map* etc. have a look at your text and **teaching point x** in particular. We're going to do a quick re-cap together on **teaching point x** as we could all do with a bit more practice.'

## BASIC SKILLS

Sadly, I believe that the teaching of basic skills, such as grammar, punctuation and spelling is in decline. There are many reasons for this, not least of which is the mistaken belief that, in Scotland, *Curriculum for Excellence* is not about that 'old-fashioned stuff'—it's about skills, not content and 'drill and kill'; it's about being a 'well-rounded' individual.

Well, I'm sorry, but you can't be a well-rounded individual if you don't have basic skills. Within *Curriculum for Excellence*, spelling, grammar, handwriting and punctuation are all mentioned and should be taught in our classrooms: they are the tools we need for reading and writing.

For me, basic skills are always on the agenda, whether or not I mention them in the 'success criteria'. If we don't correct, support, model and teach our children how these tools can make a difference to our communication, then who will? Basic skills are our job; they are our duty. Our

children would be terribly disadvantaged without them.

How do basic skills fit into *Reflective Reading*? For *Short Read*, you could create a *Blankety Blank* that makes a point e.g. remove only the verbs, adverbs, or adjectives.

During the *'Explore Some More'* on your *Task Map* you might have a question about writer's craft skills, figurative language or punctuation. When we were studying the Victorians as our project, I had one group reading *Peter Pan*. (Another group was reading an adapted version of *Sherlock Holmes* from a reading scheme, and another group were on reading books that were not linked in any way—sometimes you won't have the resources to make those connections and that's OK.) J.M. Barrie's writing is full of semi-colons and he frequently uses personification (when you describe non-humans or inanimate objects as if they were human e.g. the candles were flickering and dancing) so we were able to study these in context, consider their use and their effect.

Sometimes though, when it comes to what our children actually need in terms of practice, reinforcement or teaching, there might not be an obvious text that springs to mind, or to hand. By all means, look for links and opportunities to address needs through texts—**but if they are not forthcoming, then teach them instead.** Do not be afraid of direct teaching; it is your friend. Go to the front of the class, teach for ten minutes. Tell everyone whatever it is they need to know about apostrophes, practise/practice, number/ amount, less/fewer, ellipses, paragraphing, done it, seen it, 'could of/should of' etc. etc.

## BOOK BANDS ARE NOT YOUR FRIEND

For years, book bands have been used to classify reading books as part of reading schemes for schools, in order to help teachers find the 'right' book for each child. But did you ever wonder what this 'grading' is based on? Is this book pink, lime or lemon with blue dots? How do *they* know?

Book banding originates from *Reading Recovery* a reading intervention programme developed by Marie Clay in the 1970s. Its efficacy has been questioned by researchers for many years and it is now no longer funded in its country of origin, New Zealand. (It is however still present and paid for in the UK, including Scotland, and America.)

In their book, *Excellence and equity in literacy education: the case of New Zealand* (2015) Chapman and Turner conclude that *Reading Recovery*:

***'should be dropped and replaced by a more contemporary, research-based, reading intervention approach, together with more effective literacy instruction in children's first year of schooling'.***

Despite this, *Reading Recovery* continues to be used and book bands pervade classrooms and educational publishers' offerings. Many teachers are unaware of these origins and the faulty logic with which books are grouped or 'banded'. The book band grading system is simply based on factors such as the length of words, sentences and texts, the range of punctuation used, the size of print, the number of words/sentences on a page and the number of pages in a book.

***Book banding does not take into consideration at all the very thing that enables children to read in the first place: their phonics knowledge.***

Just because a word is long, it doesn't follow that it is difficult to read or understand. The word *bananarama* contains ten letters, which could be considered long. But you will be able to read it easily if you have already encountered *b, a, n, r,* and *m.*

Book bands rely on books which contain high levels of repetition and predictable text, this means they can often be quite boring to read. Throw in handfuls of common or 'tricky' words, sight words, multi-cueing and guessing— and you have a recipe for reading that, in the early stages at least, will do more harm than good. As already outlined in Chapter 2, decodable reading books are the solution to this; they enable children to read independently and to apply the specific knowledge and skills as they are taught in class. This provides a confident start and, along with a high quality phonics programme, can help secure rapid reading progress.

Happily, all of the main educational publishers now offer decodable books or phonics strands in their reading schemes—make sure that in the early years, certainly P1-P2/P3 (YR-Y1/Y2) and for struggling readers, that this is what you are using. Once children can read, decodable material is no longer required—the training wheels are off and they will be free readers, which will enable them to read anything that interests them.

Now that we know the grading system behind book bands, we can consider our reading groups from P3/P4 (Y2/Y3)

'The time has come,' the Walrus said,
'To talk of many things:
Of shoes and ships and sealing-wax
Of cabbages and kings
And why the sea is boiling hot
And whether pigs have wings.'


From The Walrus and the Carpenter
Through the Looking-Glass
Lewis Carroll

onwards with a fresh perspective. Do we really need 3, 4 or 5 reading groups? If everyone can read, then the answer is in fact 'no'.

Look at the books each group is reading and compare them. Is there a huge difference between them? Or is it simply the content, the number of words, sentences to a page or the number of pages in a book? Could you swap them around? Could you amalgamate two groups into one bigger group? If you're unsure, as an experiment, try swapping books to see how the children cope.

I'm not saying book bands are entirely useless. What they do provide at this stage in school, is a way of managing books and a clear pathway of progression—but they are simply an organisational tool and should be seen as such.

More often than not, reconsidering your reading groups and their books, results in the realisation that actually, you could definitely manage with fewer groups. An exciting prospect! The only problem is, you will then discover that you only have 6 copies of each book. In fact, your whole school reading system is most probably resourced in such a way as to enforce differentiation.

If the number of books you have is dictating your classroom practice, as opposed to a real educational reason or need—the diagnosis is not good: you have an urgent resourcing problem. Sorry.

The prognosis however, is great. With time, more books and more appropriate groups, everyone will feel the benefits of more focussed, rather than fragmented, teaching and practice.

## CLASSROOM ORGANISATION

How your organise your classroom and your jotters is really a personal decision, but here are some suggestions that might work for you.

Have one jotter for your extended writing that you do on a Friday (or whenever), this might be your *Big Writing* jotter, or similar. For everything else classed as English/Language, I used large jotters (that had one page lined and one page blank to each spread) and called them our *Reflective Reading Journals*. You could print out the black and white *Comprehension Compass*, ask children to colour in their own version and stick it on the front.

Other things that could be included or stuck inside the inside flaps of the jotters include:

- **Reading Record** (page 128)
- **Word Collector** (page 144)
- **Child Friendly Assessment Booklets**

Why not add some headings to pages at the back of the jotter, to note items of interest? Children could collect:

- **Favourite Quotes**
- **Book Log** (list of books read)
- **Writer's Craft Spotter** (similes, metaphors, personification etc.)

## My Word Collector

**Reflective Reading**

Name [                    ]  Class [                    ]

WOW Words, tricky words, new words, effective words, interesting words...
This is the place to collect them! Happy Word Hunting!

| Collected Word | Meaning/Definition |
|---|---|
|  |  |
|  |  |
|  |  |
|  |  |
|  |  |
|  |  |
|  |  |
|  |  |
|  |  |
|  |  |
|  |  |
|  |  |
|  |  |
|  |  |
|  | READING ON DISPLAY |

In classrooms, we always tend to have writing on display somewhere; reading is often forgotten as we don't have a tangible 'product' from reading as we do with writing. As you will be reading lots of different texts over the course of a term, and a full session, it's good to have a reminder of all of these texts, to look back on and refer to. This can be as simple as taking a copy of the front page of all books that are read and displaying them on a wall, door, or washing line.

Another display related to reading is one I had in my class called *Newsround*. (Or to bring this more up-to-date you could call it a *Flash Briefing* or something.) Every Monday morning, we would have a quick news round-up. Using a rota system, three children would 'read' us the news, with a local, national and international story that had caught their eye.

## HAVE A HYGILLIT CLASSROOM

Do you know that feeling when it's cold and dark outside and you're all tucked up warm and cosy inside with your slippers on, a book in hand, and a hot chocolate? In Denmark, they have a word for this feeling which I love: *hygge*. Pronounced *'hoo-gah',* there are whole books devoted to this subject. I think we can all benefit from more hygge moments in our lives, and in our classrooms too.

*Hygge* describes perfectly that feeling that you have when as a class you are all enthralled and engrossed in your latest class novel. Reality is suspended and we are somewhere else, feeling a unique sense of connection through the shared experience of story.

To capitalise on and increase this

special feeling, which will send the very important message that reading time is a good time, there are some things we could consider adding to our story times.

How about a special story blanket? When it's story time, everyone gathers on the blanket. If you're crafty, you could get your class to knit, crochet or sew, individual squares to build a special class patchwork quilt. If you're aiming for eco-school accreditation you could even make a rag rug out of old t-shirts.

Not crafty? Buy a picnic blanket or a cheap quilt instead. Use it at story time, but also at Golden Time. Set up a *Poetry Picnic* or a *Comic-Con* on your blanket— put out reading material that is new or extra interesting to get your customers queuing up.

Where did stories really start? Around the fire. Get hold of a silk flame fire, or a special lamp. (Or get someone handy to build you a pretend campfire out of logs, complete with red bulb. The *Guides* and *Scouts* among you will know what I mean.)

Install a reading tent if you have room; let groups have turns completing their work in it. Revamp your class library and refresh your reading corner. Instead of extension activities, offer reading in the tent, corner or school library as a reward for completing work, to show you value reading.

I love gimmicks; they create an atmosphere that everyone wants to be part of. Remember though that these must be supported by real teaching; have the glitz and glamour, but make sure that underneath, lessons have got guts.

## ROLLING OUT REFLECTIVE READING

So, what happens now? Hopefully, you've been trying out tasks and activities as we've been going along. If not, I hope you're raring to go! The best advice I can give you is 'suck it and see'.

Ideally, you'll be implementing this as a whole-school initiative, or perhaps you're going to try it out in your own classroom to see how it goes, before persuading colleagues to join you.

### START SMALL

Simply focus on one aspect of *Reflective Reading* at a time. Begin by completing the *'Cultivating a Reading Culture: Self-Evaluation'* as a staff. This should kick-start discussion about what you are already doing well—and where things could be improved.

*Short Read* is easiest to implement. Get all staff to try out a *Short Read* activity in class, then share experiences, observe lessons and discuss successes and any issues. Where possible, have stage partners working together (or at least planning together) to save on workload.

Encourage colleagues to implement ERIC, DEAR or BEAR time every day and to read to their class every day for fun—this can be a chapter book or a picture book or even a poem—no serious work or questioning required—this is for enjoyment and engagement with reading.

Once *Short Read* is underway, it is time to dive into *Long Read*. For best results, begin with a short/slim novel (e.g. *Esio Trot, Iron Man, The Twits*); you can read to the whole class, or use an audio book. For the activities, you will only need to make one *Task Map* for the week as everyone can use it in their mixed ability groups. (N.B. *Long Read* is normally in ability groupings—here we simply want to introduce the *Task Map* concept.)

You may wish to do a two-week block as a whole school—where all classes will study a novel. Classes could present at assembly about their books and if they enjoyed them.

Provide demonstration lessons to reassure colleagues. Create a shared digital resource area (such as a shared drive) using materials from the download, from *The Teaching Trunk* on *The Learning Zoo,* along with your own creations.

Where possible, buy in new books—even picture books at first, that could be used across the stages—to motivate and enthuse teachers and children. Review all reading materials in the school from the library to reading corners to reading schemes—ensure that you have recent, relevant, high quality, high interest texts of all kinds on offer—this can be an on-going project.

Perhaps this book has raised some thorny issues for your school. Consider your phonics provision and reading materials. Does every teacher know how to teach a child to read, write and spell? Is differentiation solving problems in your school, or is it adding to them? Are basic skills still being taught? Who are the children that are at risk of reading failure—what will you do about them?

References and further reading suggestions are provided in the appendix; this could be a good place to begin further research.

We hope that this book has helped you examine your reading comprehension practice in more detail and has offered some inspiration, ideas and food for thought.

We'd love to hear about the impact that *Reflective Reading* has in your class and your school. If you have comments, questions or something to share, tweet us or use the hashtag #reflectivereading. You can also email us on hello@ thelearningzoo.co.uk—or find us on Facebook, where Jeffrey posts now and again.

But perhaps most important of all, we wish you improvement and progress. Have fun reading to your class, sharing stories, words and knowledge; making memories that will last a lifetime.

For now, we'd like to take our own advice and leave you with something warm and fuzzy—a poem. It's to remind us what our children are missing out on, if we don't help them all become life-long readers.

Stay curious,

*Anne & Jeffrey x*

*Jeffrey & Anne @ LZ HQ*

*(Anne is the one on the right)*

### Bees Wings and Spiders Ankles

little, black spiders' ankles
on white, take flight
I see
goats and pigs and bears by three
tigers coming round for tea
houses made of gingerbread
grannies all tucked up in bed
*what big eyes you have grandma*
pusses in bootses; cats in hats
moles and toads and river rats
planets, kingdoms; near and far
woods where all the wild things are

I see me
floating on the wings of bees
stories buzzing in the trees
taster of porridge, maker of maps
climber of beanstalks, setter of traps
traveller in time, wisher of wells
puller of turnips, caster of spells
finder of treasure, captain of boats
kisser of frogs, defender of moats
driver of rockets and stagecoach wagons
tamer of wolves, slayer of dragons

I am: built of books;
word breather
heart hearer
soul feeder
I. Am. Reader.

# Appendix

## JANEY ROSS

# Reflective Reading Case Study

**Class Teacher, Janey Ross, describes how she went about implementing the Reflective Reading approach in her Primary 2 (Year 1) classroom. She considers the impact elements of the methodology have had on her own practice and on the children she teaches.**

I know it's perhaps clichéd to say, but the Reflective Reading methodology really has helped to change my practice and it has had (and continues to have!) a very positive impact on learners in my classroom.

I was keen to implement EVERYTHING I had learned from Anne as soon after the training as possible—I was motivated and enthused and knew my learners would be too.

The first thing I wanted to do was to create a 'reading rich' classroom. I audited the reading material and reading resources I already had using the self-evaluation. I wanted to surround the children with high quality and motivating reading material (of all genres) and I wanted them to be able to access these for pleasure on a regular basis. I liaised with our local library service and ordered book boxes which were packed full of props and puppets and I also purchased a listening centre with headphones. From this every Tuesday became 'Choose-Day' (when children were allowed to choose their own books for reading time) in P2: this was an instant hit and became the children's 'best bit' on our weekly timetable!

We used this opportunity to be creative with texts; the children created story stones, sticker stories and used reading sticks, costumes and props. We used Lego to recreate favourite scenes and characters from books. Sometimes our P5 reading buddies would come along to share the joy! It immersed the children in a reading-rich environment; they were free to choose their own text and able to engage with texts which they wouldn't normally choose or have been exposed to.

In addition to this, I read to the children everyday and we would pick out and 'magpie' the 'best bits' from books, collecting and discussing WOW words which we would talk about explicitly and try and use in our conversations and in our writing. Fridays were reserved for fairy-tales (Fairy-Tale Friday) which we always settle down to on our story blanket. These subtle but highly effective 'tweaks' in my practice have helped to build a love for reading, and a culture and ethos where reading for pleasure is not only encouraged but valued too.

Reflective Reading has helped me to structure the children's weekly reading, systematically and progressively, and has allowed me to plan for both core reading and an additional longer read.

I now have a plethora of techniques at my fingertips to teach reading explicitly, which are fun and motivating. As a practitioner I am enabling high quality learning experiences which promote higher order thinking and greater engagement. It's notable that the children are concentrated, creative, energetic and persistent in their reading activities. Having used this methodology in two very different school contexts, I can confidently say that it works and it has a tangible impact!

The TexTplorers activities help me to focus my learners on reading skills. I've had success with Picture It, Blankety Blank, Choral Reading, Spot the Silly Word and Task Mats. The children particularly enjoyed The Cereal Box Task Mat—even those who have been somewhat reluctant to engage were up for this challenge! It was enlightening to hear them comment that it was *amazing that we're using cereal boxes for our reading today and not a reading book!* This prompted me to use more 'real life' contexts for reading activities.

Working in mixed ability trios has helped to foster a very cooperative and supportive classroom culture where a growth mind-set can be nurtured and developed. To be effective and have the greatest impact, every lesson needs to be 'reflective' (just like it says on the tin!) Questions are posed by Jeffrey (the Giraffe) which allow the children the chance to think about and talk about their own learning. This dialogue is embedded throughout and over time the children in my class have become more self-aware, more able to talk about their own learning and consider their own next steps.

I changed our 'reading records' to Reflective Reading ones so that parents could talk to their children about their FASE. Parents were very positive as it was facilitating focused conversations and helping to support their children's reading at home too.

I think the comment from a parent of a little girl who used to be a very reluctant reader sums up the success of the approach: *'Thank you so much for your help and support with A's reading. As you know I've not been able to help support A's her and to see her progress and feel more confident means the world to me. Just a wee present so you can enjoy reading as much as A does now!'* (Enclosed was a reading light!) Reading this made me emotional as A's mum had previously found it challenging to support her daughter at home.

Being a learner myself and exploring reading pedagogy has impacted my practice and my pupils' learning in such a positive way. I now have a strong desire to help others love teaching reading, in my school setting and beyond. And of course, I'm going to keep learning—and keep reading too.

## ANNE GLENNIE
# A Journey to the Dark Side: from Phonics Phobic to Phonics Fanatic

I don't remember how I learned to read, probably because I didn't struggle with it. I was lucky. I grew up on a council housing estate—or scheme—as we prefer to refer to it in Scotland, but I had everything that we would now consider to be the ideal 'pre-five home learning environment'. My many memories include tent building in the living room, making mud pies and petal perfume, digging up worms, and swinging endlessly on my blue swing in the garden. I spent a lot of time outside, with friends, or with my two imaginary dogs—Toby and Sheba. But I also remember books. I had my very own bookcase which housed my Ladybird library, in my own playroom. I would spend hours reading them, sometimes even in the middle of the night, by the landing light.

My mum read to me too. *The Tiger Who Came to Tea* became an instant favourite, but so did another less well-known story: *A Brother for Momoko*. I was four when my mum read this to me (preparing me for the fact that I was no longer going to be an only child). I remember the story, the pictures, and my mum's voice—her intonation when she read to me. When the baby comes home from the hospital, he is *'tiny, soft and warm.'* And so was my brother. He moved into my playroom, and despite a vigorous campaign, my parents called him Brian, instead of my choice: Toby.

My love of books and reading was nurtured at school in every class. But my favourite teacher, Mrs Clarke, is the one that introduced me to *Charlotte's Web* and *A Gift from Winklesea*. It was these shared reading experiences that propelled me into teaching. I wanted to recreate those magical, memorable moments and share the power of words and stories with every child in my class.

This romantic notion was quickly quashed. When I started teaching, the curriculum at the time in Scotland was the now abandoned 5-14. Strict timetables dictated how many minutes were to be devoted to each subject area per week. I remember asking a colleague 'But when do we get to do the class novel?' Only to be told. 'We don't do that anymore.' Undeterred, I simply used the ten 'extra' minutes per day for this purpose. I think I've read *A Gift from Winklesea* to every class I've ever had, regardless of age or stage; it's a great story. We should never underestimate the power we have as teachers, to influence not just learning, but entire lives. Thank you, Mrs Clarke.

Today, I'm no longer in the classroom, but I still get to share my passion for reading through my work as a consultant. I developed *Reflective Reading*, a methodology that focuses on comprehension, higher order thinking skills and reading for pleasure, with practical ideas and materials that teachers can use in the classroom. However, I began to realise that although I could talk forever about engagement, enjoyment and 'getting under the skin' of a text, I lacked real knowledge and expertise in the fundamentals of reading acquisition. If someone was to ask me 'How should we teach children to read?' I'd be lost. I didn't know the 'right' answer.

As a teacher, there can be nothing more shameful than admitting that you don't know how to teach a child to read. While in the classroom, it was an area I'd managed to avoid—I was a self-styled 'upper stages' teacher. Partly because I love those stages and the opportunity for in-depth learning and reading, but partly because I was afraid of the huge responsibility of teaching a class of younger children to read. How had I managed to qualify as a primary teacher without this essential knowledge? For a while, I kept my shameful secret to myself, believing that I must have slept in the day 'Teaching Reading' was covered in lectures. I couldn't ignore though, the fact that I had just identified a major personal, professional development need. If I was training teachers, I needed to be sure that whatever I was telling them, whatever questions were being asked, that I was providing the correct answers.

Three years ago, as part of my quest to find out how to do my job, I read another book that changed my life: *Early Reading Instruction: What Science Really Tells Us About How to Teach Reading* by Diane McGuinness. I found out about it, quite by chance, online. I'm a keen Twitter user; it keeps me up to date with education news, motivational quotes and cat videos. It's also brilliant for pedagogical debate; night or day the fires of 'the reading wars' are being fanned, as someone somewhere will be arguing about phonics.

Phonics wasn't something I had previously thought a lot about. It wasn't necessary to my practice in Primary 6 or 7 (Year 5 or 6)—or so I believed. The few opinions I had about phonics, had mostly been absorbed though listening to wiser colleagues and teachers, staffroom discussion, and Michael Rosen. Type 'phonics' into the search engine of my brain, and the result would be phrases such as 'barking at print', 'first, fast and only', 'one size doesn't fit all', 'there's more to reading than phonics' and 'drill and kill'. I certainly didn't want to have anything to do with a pedagogy that would destroy the very thing I was trying to achieve—a love of reading.

But when I read Diane McGuinness's book, the scales fell from my eyes. This was a game-changer. Here was undeniable, compelling, unequivocal scientific proof that systematic phonics was the most effective way to teach all children to read. Indeed, I was late to the party; three major international enquiries into reading had already established this conclusion —one of them being The Rose Review (*Independent review of the teaching of early reading, Final Report, Jim Rose,* March 2006).

Everything I'd previously believed about phonics was wrong. Of course 'there is more to reading than phonics'; advocates of the approach not only want children to be able to read, for pleasure and for learning, but phonics was a means to an end—a way of ensuring that all children could access text. Comprehension is the ultimate goal, why else do we read, if not to understand the writer's message? But to understand the message, first you have to be able read it. I now believe that it takes three things to build a reader: motivation, meaning, and mechanics;

none is sufficient on its own. It doesn't matter how many wonderful books you surround children with, or how engaging and exciting you make reading—if they can't decode the words on the page, then they will fail. No one can read for pleasure if they can't read.

The sad reality is, that phonics has a massive PR problem, perpetuated by people who are no doubt well-meaning, but misinformed. When these people are high profile academics, authors, and journalists who are openly anti-phonics, their influence can be difficult to overcome. In Scotland, despite constant talk of how teaching should be 'research-informed', our own curriculum does not take this on-board. With regards to beginning reading instruction, Scotland is firmly in the mixed methods camp. We do teach phonics... alongside sight words, letter names and a myriad of unhelpful multi-cueing strategies and a cupboard full of 'look and say' books.

Whole language rhetoric is alive and well, with children being encouraged to 'look at the first letter', 'look at the last letter' (yes, really!) and 'look at the picture and guess'. (Pictures and context of course must be used for comprehension—just not for reading or guessing individual words.) The most helpful advice of all 'sound it out' appears only towards the end of a long list. Reading is not about memorisation, nor is it about guessing.

Simply teaching children about our language, the alphabetic code and how it works, means that all the clues required for reading are right there, in the words on the page. Knowledge of letters and sounds, coupled with the skills of sounding out and blending—or phonics—is the only strategy beginning

readers need to get the words off the page. It's the one we use as adults too, when we're faced with a word we don't know. (Try reading this if you don't believe me: atelerix albiventris—which is the Latin name for an African pygmy hedgehog, in case you were wondering) And as if that wasn't enough, that same letter/ sound knowledge is what we need for spelling too; systematic synthetic phonics delivers for both reading and spelling—it's a win-win.

The real irony though, is that one of the main studies into the effectiveness of systematic synthetic phonics was carried out here in Clackmannanshire, by Johnston and Watson. This study has gained international interest and acclaim, it features in Diane McGuinness's book, and six pages of the Rose Review cover what Sir Jim Rose and his team discovered when they visited Scotland. We do not appear to be learning the lessons, even from our own research.

I also discovered that I wasn't the only one who had missed out on instruction in the nuts and bolts of reading instruction. I regularly ask teachers on my courses if they were taught how to teach reading during their teacher training. Shockingly, the majority of teachers in Scotland have had no input on the subject of beginning reading instruction or phonics. To be clear, this is not the fault of teachers, for me, the blame lies with teacher training institutions, Education Scotland and the Scottish Government. I have written to my MSP, our previous Education Secretary and the GTCS (General Teaching Council for Scotland) about this matter, to no avail.

My new passion for phonics has left some of my colleagues puzzled. Some have chosen to distance themselves from me, uncomfortable with my 'controversial' approach to teaching reading. Working outside the Scottish education system, as an independent consultant, means I am free to challenge Education Scotland and our approaches to literacy teaching and assessment. This is not a method I'd recommend if you're looking to make friends, rather than enemies. Nevertheless, I do believe that, however difficult, the path I have chosen is the correct one.

Yes, I am a phonics fanatic. I have become evangelical. I can't help it. People say that there are no silver bullets in education, but I think systematic synthetic phonics comes pretty close. A method of teaching reading that has scientific backing and is proven to be effective for all children—especially those who are disadvantaged because of socio-economic factors, have English as a second language, or struggle with dyslexic-type difficulties—is one worth fighting for.

Knowing that the research is on my side gives me confidence. Believing that no child should have to experience reading failure, and all that entails for their future life chances, is what gives me the courage to keep going. I may have crossed over to what many view 'as the dark side', but for the first time in my teaching career, I feel truly enlightened. My only wish is that I converted years ago.

Originally published in the **NATE Teaching English Primary Matters** magazine (Summer Edition, July 2017)

**National Association for the Teaching of English**
www.nate.org.uk
@NATE feed

**TexTplorers** Blankety Blank: ANSWERS **Reflective Reading**

Extract from *Alice's Adventures in Wonderland* Chapter I: Down the Rabbit-Hole

*Alice has followed the White Rabbit and fallen down an enormous rabbit-hole, landing at the bottom.*

Suddenly she came upon a little three–legged table, all made of solid glass; there was nothing on it except a tiny golden **_key_**, and Alice's first thought was that it might belong to one of the doors of the hall; but, alas! either the locks were **_too_** large, or the key was too small, but at any rate it would not **_open_** any of them. However, on the second time round, she came upon a low curtain she had not noticed before, and behind it was a little door about fifteen inches **_high_**: she tried the little **_golden_** key in the lock, and to her great **_delight_** it fitted!

Alice opened the door and found that it led into a small passage, not much larger than a rat–hole: she **_knelt_** down and looked along the passage into the loveliest garden you ever saw. How she **_longed_** to get out of that dark hall, and wander about among those beds of bright **_flowers_** and those **_cool_** fountains, but she could not even get her head through the doorway; 'and even if my head would go through,' thought poor Alice, 'it would be of very little use without my **_shoulders_**. Oh, how I wish I could shut up like a telescope! I think I could, if I only know how to begin.' For, you see, so many out–of–the–way things had happened lately, that Alice had begun to think that very few things indeed were really impossible.

There seemed to be no use in waiting by the little door, so she went back to the table, half **_hoping_** she might find another key on it, or at any rate a book of rules for shutting people up like **_telescopes_**: this time she found a little bottle on it, ('which certainly was not here before,' said Alice,) and round the neck of the bottle was a paper label, with the words '**_DRINK_** ME' beautifully printed on it in large **_letters_**.

It was all very well to say 'Drink me,' but the wise little Alice was not going to do THAT in a hurry. 'No, I'll look first,' she said, 'and see whether it's marked "**_poison_**" or not'; for she had read several nice little histories about children who had got burnt, and eaten up by wild **_beasts_** and other unpleasant things, all because they WOULD not remember the simple rules their friends had taught them: such as, that a red–hot poker will **_burn_** you if you hold it too long; and that if you cut your finger VERY deeply with a knife, it usually **_bleeds_**; and she had never forgotten that, if you drink much from a bottle marked 'poison,' it is almost certain to disagree with you, **_sooner_** or later.

However, this bottle was NOT marked 'poison,' so Alice **_ventured_** to taste it, and finding it very nice, (it had, in fact, a sort of mixed flavour of cherry–tart, custard, pine–apple, roast **_turkey_**, toffee, and hot buttered **_toast_**,) she very soon finished it off.

'What a **_curious_** feeling!' said Alice; 'I must be **_shutting_** up like a telescope.'

Source: Lewis Carroll (1865) *Alice's Adventures in Wonderland* London, England: Macmillan Publishing Co.

# TexTplorers    Blankety Blank: ANSWERS    Reflective Reading

Extract from *Alice's Adventures in Wonderland* Chapter I: Down the Rabbit-Hole

***Alice has followed the White Rabbit and fallen down an enormous rabbit-hole, landing at the bottom.***

Suddenly she came upon a little three–legged table, all made of solid glass; there was nothing on it except a tiny golden ***key***, and Alice's first thought was that it might belong to one of the doors of the hall; but, alas! either the locks were ***too*** large, or the key was too small, but at any rate it would not ***open*** any of them. However, on the second time round, she came upon a low curtain she had not noticed before, and behind it was a little door about fifteen inches ***high***: she tried the little ***golden*** key in the lock, and to her great ***delight*** it fitted!

Alice opened the door and found that it led into a small passage, not much larger than a rat–hole: she ***knelt*** down and looked along the passage into the loveliest garden you ever saw. How she ***longed*** to get out of that dark hall, and wander about among those beds of bright ***flowers*** and those ***cool*** fountains, but she could not even get her head through the doorway; 'and even if my head would go through,' thought poor Alice, 'it would be of very little use without my ***shoulders***. Oh, how I wish I could shut up like a telescope! I think I could, if I only know how to begin.' For, you see, so many out–of–the–way things had happened lately, that Alice had begun to think that very few things indeed were really impossible.

There seemed to be no use in waiting by the little door, so she went back to the table, half ***hoping*** she might find another key on it, or at any rate a book of rules for shutting people up like ***telescopes***: this time she found a little bottle on it, ('which certainly was not here before,' said Alice,) and round the neck of the bottle was a paper label, with the words '***DRINK*** ME' beautifully printed on it in large ***letters***.

It was all very well to say 'Drink me,' but the wise little Alice was not going to do THAT in a hurry. 'No, I'll look first,' she said, 'and see whether it's marked "***poison***" or not'; for she had read several nice little histories about children who had got burnt, and eaten up by wild ***beasts*** and other unpleasant things, all because they WOULD not remember the simple rules their friends had taught them: such as, that a red–hot poker will ***burn*** you if you hold it too long; and that if you cut your finger VERY deeply with a knife, it usually ***bleeds***; and she had never forgotten that, if you drink much from a bottle marked 'poison,' it is almost certain to disagree with you, ***sooner*** or later.

However, this bottle was NOT marked 'poison,' so Alice ***ventured*** to taste it, and finding it very nice, (it had, in fact, a sort of mixed flavour of cherry–tart, custard, pine–apple, roast ***turkey***, toffee, and hot buttered ***toast***,) she very soon finished it off.

'What a ***curious*** feeling!' said Alice; 'I must be ***shutting*** up like a telescope.'

Source: Lewis Carroll (1865) *Alice's Adventures in Wonderland* London, England: Macmillan Publishing Co.

## TexTplorers Blankety Blank: ANSWERS: Why Children are as Good as Gold at Christmas

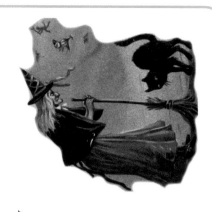

Are you sick of getting *__socks__* or new pyjamas at Christmas? If you lived in Iceland you would certainly be grateful if your presents contained something to *__wear__*. Even a *__hideous__* Christmas jumper would be a welcome gift because it would prevent you from being eaten by Jólakötturinn the Christmas Cat!

Old Icelandic folklore states that every Icelander must receive a new piece of *__clothing__* for Christmas or they will find themselves in mortal danger. An enormous black cat is said to *__prowl__* around the snowy streets on Christmas Eve, *__peering__* through windows, looking for people who haven't kept this simple rule. Not wearing something new on Christmas Eve? *__Jólakötturinn__* will eat you!

However, perhaps worse still is Jólakötturinn's owner: Gryla. Traditional tales tell of a giant ogress, who is part troll, part animal, that lives up in the *__mountains__* with her cat, her third husband and her thirteen children. At Christmas Gryla and her sons, who are also known as the Yuletide Lads, come down from the mountains. Gryla looks for naughty children that she can *__capture__* and put into her *__cauldron__* to boil them up and eat them. The only way to escape this terrible *__fate__*, is for the children to apologise for their bad behaviour.

Perhaps one of the nicer Icelandic tales concerns Gryla's sons. The Yuletide Lads are actually like thirteen *__Santas__* or Father Christmases. Icelandic children put a *__shoe__* in their bedroom window each evening for 13 days before Christmas. Every night, one Yuletide Lad visits, leaving sweets and small presents—or rotting potatoes—in their shoe, depending on if they have been *__naughty__* or nice.

Although these tales are only stories, Gryla, her sons and the Christmas Cat ensure that Icelandic children everywhere are as good as *__gold__* at Christmas.

Reflective Reading

# TeXTplorers

## Spot the Silly Word: Roald Dahl's Early Life

### Early life

1   Roald Dahl was born in 1916 in Cardiff, Wales to Norwegian parents, Harald and Sofie Dahl. Dahl's family moved from Norway and settled in Cardiff in the 1880s. He **spoke** Norwegian at home with his parents and sisters. Roald Dahl attended the Cathedral School in Llandaff in **_1923_**.

Photo credit: Hans van Dijk / Anefo

5   Aged eight, Roald and four of his **_friends_** were caned by the headmaster after putting a dead **_mouse_** in a jar of sweets at the local sweet shop, which was owned by a 'mean and loathsome' old woman called Mrs Pratchett. This was known amongst the five boys as the 'Great Mouse Plot of 1923'.

### School life

Roald went to St Peter's School in Weston-super-Mare in 1925 and then Repton public school in 1929. He was very **_homesick_** and wrote to his mother almost every day.

10   During his years at Repton, the chocolate company Cadbury would send boxes of new **_chocolates_** to the school to be tested by the pupils. Roald Dahl used to dream of **_inventing_** a new chocolate bar that would win the praise of Mr Cadbury himself, and this provided the inspiration for him to write his third **_gorilla_** for children, Charlie and the Chocolate **_Factory_**.

15   Roald was very tall, reaching 6'6" in adult life, and he was good at sports. He also had an **_interest_** in photography. In childhood and adolescence, he spent his summer **_holidays_** in Norway.

Source: Text adapted from Roald Dahl, http://en.wikipedia.org/w/index.php?title=Roald_Dahl&oldid=644359001 This work is licensed under a Creative Commons Attribution-ShareAlike 4.0 International License http://creativecommons.org/licenses/by-sa/4.0/

## Literacy and English: Listening and Talking

These documents have been created to assist with evaluating, planning, tracking and assessing Listening and Talking. They are designed to be used in conjunction with the *Reflective Reading* materials, in particular, the CfE Reading Tracker and the Child Friendly Assessment Booklets. Written with reference to the Experiences and Outcomes, the documents should help ensure teachers are familiar with the requirements set out in *Curriculum for Excellence*.

Within Literacy and English there is a natural overlap between the skills of Reading, Writing, Listening and Talking. Teachers using reading approaches (such as Reflective Reading) which involve group work with a focus on discussion, as well as the higher order thinking skills, will find that they are automatically addressing many of the Experiences and Outcomes for Listening and Talking in their day-to-day planning, teaching and learning. Special consideration must be given however to the organiser 'Creating texts' to ensure that children are given ample, relevant opportunities to plan, write and participate in group discussions/debates and solo talks or presentations, in a variety of curricular areas.

## Progression through the Levels and Assessment

Despite being arranged in levels, from Early to Fourth, the descriptions of knowledge/skills in Listening and Talking Experiences and Outcomes are all very similar, with only minor word changes at certain levels, and as such they do not provide a clear progression or expectation at each level. This is because differentiation and progression is achieved through consideration of other aspects which affect the breadth and challenge of tasks in Listening and Talking. For example:

- increasing challenge of context, subject matter or issues
- level of teacher input, support and guidance with increasing independence
- sophistication in vocabulary and techniques used
- increase in length, detail, complexity of talk
- increasing confidence and enthusiasm for sharing experiences through talk
- ability to express an increasingly complex personal response with justification

For this reason, the two observational assessment sheets that are provided, the *Group Discussion Assessment* and the *Solo Talk Assessment*, are the same for every level. It will be for the teacher to decide, using their professional judgement, if a particular statement can be given a tick, dot or a cross.

N.B. some statements may not apply depending on the context—these can simply be marked with a dash—or 'n/a' (not applicable).

In this way, the same assessment sheet can be used whether listening to a 'Show and Tell' style talk in P1, right up to a *Dragons' Den* style presentation in the upper stages. This will help provide consistency across the school and ensure that all teachers share a common language about Listening and Talking. The sheets are not designed to be used to attribute marks or levels to individual children, rather, they should be used to highlight strengths and points for development at an individual level, as well as whole class level.

It is recommended that at least four assessments are carried out per session, ideally one each term. These should involve group discussion/debates as well as solo talks or presentations and should ensure variety in terms of purpose (to inform, persuade, entertain etc.), audience (group, own class, younger class, whole-school, parents, invited guests etc.), curricular area, subject matter and format (use of technology/formal or informal situation).

'*Tick the Talk*' Peer Assessment strips are also provided for group talk and solo talk purposes. All of these are available to download.

## Talk the Talk: Creating Opportunities for Listening and Talking

This page is designed to encourage collegiate discussion, evaluation and reflection on opportunities for listening and talking within the school, and individual classrooms. It is a useful aid to review progress and identify action points on a termly basis.

### Whole School Issues

| | | | | |
|---|---|---|---|---|
| We take part in or organise events and competitions that promote spoken language such as debating competitions, speech making competitions, poetry recitals and presentations. | | | | |
| Visitors, such as authors or artists, and community members, including parents, regularly visit the school or classes to talk about, discuss or present on subjects of interest. | | | | |
| Assemblies include regular opportunities for children to contribute through asking and answering questions, presenting or performing or sharing recent successes or experiences in or out of class. | | | | |
| We encourage all children, at all stages, to speak in full and proper (extended) sentences. We may have adopted a visual sign to remind everyone about this school routine. (such as BSL sign for 'more') | | | | |
| We watch and discuss events that focus on listening to a speaker/s, such as the SBT Authors Live, footage from the Scottish Parliament, TED talks or similar. | | | | |
| We have an active Debating Club. | | | | |
| In the school, and in all classes, we value all languages, promoting and providing opportunities to speak and listen in other languages, particularly Scots and Gaelic and in our L2 and L3 languages (for 1+2 policy). | | | | |

### Teaching, Learning and Classroom Routine

| | | | | |
|---|---|---|---|---|
| I provide regular and varied opportunities for children to give or take part in group discussions, class debates, solo talks or presentations. (May be as simple as 'Show and Tell') At least one of these will be teacher assessed, with feedback given, per term. Peer/Self assessment is also in evidence. | | | | |
| Our classroom has an established listening and talking culture, which may include how we ask and answer questions. (such as hands-up/no hands-up, lollipop sticks, Shoulder Partner etc.) | | | | |
| I provide varied texts/resources to stimulate talk: 'Provocation to Talk' scene setting, objects, photos, paintings, Thunks, statements (may be philosophical in nature), audio/visual clips, films etc. | | | | |
| I provide opportunities for speaking and listening outwith the school environment. | | | | |
| I encourage discussion of topical and relevant news items, whether international or local in nature. | | | | |
| I look for opportunities to build listening and talking into every area of the curriculum. | | | | |
| Through Reflective Reading, I promote higher order thinking and discussion, including expressing opinions and answering literal, inferential and evaluative questions. Children also create and ask higher order questions of their own during reading. | | | | |
| As a class we have explored and discussed what we feel makes a good speaker and listener. This is recorded in some way (e.g. poster, wall display, list) and is easily accessible as a reminder for all. | | | | |

### Teacher as Listener and Speaker

| | | | | |
|---|---|---|---|---|
| I model respectful and appropriate speaking and listening at all times. I model correct Standard (Scottish) English, particularly in the early years and during periods of more formal, direct teaching. | | | | |
| I participate effectively in staff meetings and am able to contribute ideas and voice my opinions tactfully. I can feedback on initiatives, present ideas, give training and am confident speaking to a group of teachers (known or unknown) and leading discussions. | | | | |
| I model Talk the Talk and thinking, as well as expressing my opinions and thoughts. (*as appropriate!) | | | | |
| I listen to professional texts, such as educational podcasts or conference speeches, to help develop and inform my practice. I debate and discuss relevant issues with colleagues. | | | | |

Name:                    Class:

| | Context/Curricular Area | Audience/Purpose | Title/Topic/Theme |
|---|---|---|---|
| 1 | | | |
| 2 | | | |
| 3 | | | |
| 4 | | | |

## Delivery

| | 1 | 2 | 3 | 4 |
|---|---|---|---|---|
| I can speak clearly, at an appropriate speed and volume level, suitable for my audience. | | | | |
| I am confident in front of my audience and make (or give the impression of) eye contact. | | | | |
| I am enthusiastic about my topic and the opportunity to share it with my audience. | | | | |
| I use visual aids, such as photos or objects, where appropriate, and ensure they can be seen by my audience. | | | | |
| Where appropriate, I use technology confidently to support my talk (e.g. presentation software such as PowerPoint, clicker or microphone) or to record my talk (e.g. tablet, phone, camera). | | | | |
| My body language, including posture, gestures and facial expressions support my talk. | | | | |
| I may use more sophisticated techniques to engage the audience: using (rhetorical) questions; humour, surprise, varying the pace of my talk for effect, or the intonation/expression of my voice. | | | | |

## Content

| | 1 | 2 | 3 | 4 |
|---|---|---|---|---|
| My talk makes sense, is well-planned and ordered; making it easy for my audience to follow. | | | | |
| I articulate a number of facts, points, ideas, opinions, arguments, feelings or experiences clearly. | | | | |
| I can explain processes, concepts or ideas. | | | | |
| I identify issues and can summarise findings and/or draw conclusions. | | | | |
| I use vocabulary and language that is suitable/interesting/useful for my audience. | | | | |
| My talk is well structured with an appropriate introduction and conclusion. | | | | |
| My tone/register is suitable for the occasion i.e. formal/informal. | | | | |
| I can use presentation software (e.g. PowerPoint, Prezi, Keynote or YouTube) and design the slides/film clip to support my talk effectively. | | | | |
| My talk is interesting and/or informative and holds the attention of the audience. (in general!) | | | | |
| My talk meets its purpose i.e. to inform, persuade or entertain. | | | | |
| I can respond appropriately to, and answer effectively, questions from the audience. | | | | |
| I show good manners and thank my audience for their time and attention. | | | | |

## Notes:

| | |
|---|---|
| 1 | |
| 2 | |
| 3 | |
| 4 | |

| | Context/Curricular Area | Audience/Purpose | Title/Topic/Theme |
|---|---|---|---|
| 1 | | | |
| 2 | | | |
| 3 | | | |
| 4 | | | |

Name:          Class:          Group Discussion Assessment

## Participation and Engagement

| | 1 | 2 | 3 | 4 |
|---|---|---|---|---|
| I listen attentively, focussing on the speaker. | | | | |
| I show an active interest in the speaker, and may display any of the following: open, attentive or thoughtful expression; nodding in agreement; leaning forward to encourage speaker; smiling. | | | | |
| In a group, I show awareness of turn taking and when to talk and when to listen. | | | | |
| I articulate my points, ideas, opinions, arguments or feelings clearly. | | | | |
| I am able to justify my point of view with reasons or evidence, where appropriate. | | | | |
| I listen carefully to and consider the points made by others with an open mind. | | | | |
| I use vocabulary and language that is suitable/interesting/useful for my audience. | | | | |
| I use the language of debate*. (*refer to additional handout) | | | | |
| I ask appropriate and thoughtful questions or raise pertinent points. | | | | |
| I respond effectively to questions or points made by others. | | | | |
| I can summarise and build on others' contributions. | | | | |
| I am able to challenge, disagree or question others' contributions in a tactful way. | | | | |
| I engage respectfully with others in the group at all times and remember my manners. | | | | |
| I participate confidently and contribute effectively in a group discussion scenario. | | | | |
| I attempt to facilitate the discussion by: encouraging others to contribute; asking others to expand on their answers or ideas; praising their contributions. | | | | |
| I take a lead role in the discussion by: keeping the group on task; maintaining order; being sensible and impartial; subduing dominant voices diplomatically; playing devil's advocate to encourage talk; considering all viewpoints. | | | | |

## Notes:

| | |
|---|---|
| 1 | |
| 2 | |
| 3 | |
| 4 | |

# Reflective Listening & Talking: Early Level Planning Sheet

## Enjoyment and Choice

| | | | |
|---|---|---|---|
| I enjoy exploring and playing with the patterns and sounds of language and can use what I learn. (LIT 0-01a, LIT 0-11a, LIT 0-20a) | | | |
| I enjoy exploring and choosing stories and other texts to watch, read or listen to, and can share my likes and dislikes. (LIT 0-01b, LIT 0-11b) | | | |
| I enjoy exploring events and characters in stories and other texts, sharing my thoughts in different ways. (LIT 0-01c) | | | |
| I enjoy listening to, and joining in with, rhymes, songs and stories. | | | |
| I enjoy watching and listening to television programmes, films and audio CDs. | | | |
| I say what I like/don't like about a story or text I know. | | | |
| I can talk about what happened in a story or text, describing events and characters. | | | |
| I can re-tell stories and talk about 'What? Where? Who? When? Why? How?' | | | |

## Tools for Listening and Talking

As I listen and talk in different situations, I am learning to take turns and am developing my awareness of when to talk and when to listen. (LIT 0-02a, ENG 0-03a)

## Finding and Using Information

I listen or watch for useful or interesting information and I use this to make choices or learn new things. (LIT 0-04a)

## Understanding, analysing, evaluating

To help me understand stories and other texts, I ask questions and link what I am learning with what I already know. (LIT 0-07a, LIT 0-16a, ENG 0-17a)

## Creating Texts

Within real and imaginary situations, I share experiences and feelings, ideas and information in a way that communicates my message. (LIT 0-09a)

I enjoy exploring events and characters in stories and other texts and I use what I learn to invent my own, sharing these with others in imaginative ways. (LIT 0-09b, LIT 0-31a)

As I listen and take part in conversations and discussions, I discover new words and phrases which I use to help me express my ideas, thoughts and feelings. (LIT 0-10a)

Notes:

# Reflective Listening & Talking: First Level Planning Sheet

## Enjoyment and Choice

I regularly select and listen to or watch texts which I enjoy and find interesting, and I can say why I prefer certain sources. I regularly select subject, purpose, format and resources to create texts of my choice. (LIT 1-01a)

## Tools for Talking and Listening

When I engage with others, I know when and how to listen, when to talk, how much to say, when to ask questions and how to respond with respect. (LIT 1-02a)

## Finding and Using Information

As I listen or watch, I can identify and discuss the purpose, **key words** and main ideas of the text, and use this information for a specific purpose. (LIT 1-04a)

As I listen or watch, I am learning to **make notes under given headings** and use these to understand what I have listened to or watched and create new texts. (LIT 1-05a)

I can select ideas and relevant information, **organise these in a logical sequence and use words which will be interesting and/or useful for others**. (LIT 1-06a)

## Understanding, analysing, evaluating

I can show my understanding of what I listen to or watch by responding to and asking different kinds of questions. (LIT 1-07a)

To help me develop and informed view, **I am learning to recognise the difference between fact and** opinion. (LIT 1-08a)

## Creating Texts

When listening and talking with others for different purposes, **I can exchange information, experiences, explanations, ideas and opinions, and clarify points by asking questions or by asking others to say more**. (LIT 1-09a)

I can communicate clearly when engaging with others **within and beyond my place of learning**, using selected resources (this may include images, objects, audio, visual or digital resources) as required. (LIT 1-10a)

Notes:

## Reflective Listening & Talking: Second Level Planning Sheet
### Enjoyment and Choice

I regularly select and listen to or watch texts which I enjoy and find interesting, and I can explain why I prefer certain sources. I regularly select subject, purpose, format and resources to create texts of my choice. (LIT 2-01a)

### Tools for Talking and Listening

When I engage with others, I can respond in ways appropriate to my role, show that **I value others' contributions and use these to build on thinking**. (LIT 2-02a)

### Finding and Using Information

As I listen or watch, I can identify and discuss the purpose, main ideas **and supporting detail** contained within the text, and use this information for different purposes. (LIT 2-04a)

As I listen or watch, I can make notes, **organise these under suitable headings** and use these to understand ideas and information and create new texts, using my own words as appropriate. (LIT 2-05a)

I can select ideas and relevant information, organise these in an appropriate way for my purpose and use suitable vocabulary for my audience. (LIT 1-06a)

### Understanding, analysing, evaluating

I can show my understanding of what I listen to or watch **by responding to literal, inferential,** evaluative **and** other **types of questions, and by asking different kinds of questions on my own.** (LIT 2-07a)

To help me develop and informed view, **I can distinguish fact from opinion, and I am learning to** recognise when **my sources try to influence me and how useful these are. (**LIT 2-08a)

### Creating Texts

When listening and talking with others for different purposes, I can: share information, experiences and opinions; **explain processes and ideas; identify issues raised and summarise main points or findings**; clarify points by asking questions or by asking others to say more. (LIT 2-09a)

**I am developing confidence when engaging with others within and beyond my place of learning**. I can communicate in a clear, expressive way and **I am learning to select and organise resources independently**. (LIT 2-10a)

Notes:

## Reflective Listening & Talking: Third Level Planning Sheet

### Enjoyment and Choice

I regularly select and listen to or watch texts for enjoyment and interest, and I can express how well they meet my needs and expectations, and I can give reasons, with evidence, for my personal response. I can **regularly** select subject, purpose, format and resources to create texts of my choice, **and am developing my own style.** (LIT 3-01a)

| | | | |
|---|---|---|---|

### Tools for Talking and Listening

When I engage with others, **I can** make **a relevant contribution, encourage others to contribute and acknowledge that they have the right to hold a different opinion.** I can respond in ways appropriate to my role and use **contributions to reflect on, clarify or adapt thinking.** (LIT 3-02a)

| | | | |
|---|---|---|---|

### Finding and Using Information

As I listen or watch, I can: identify and **give an accurate account of** the purpose, and main **concerns** of the text, and **can make inferences from key statements**; **identify and** discuss **similarities and differences between** different **types of text**; use this information for different purposes. (LIT 3-04a)

| | | | |
|---|---|---|---|

As I listen or watch, I can make notes **and** organise **these to develop thinking, help retain and recall information**, explore issues and create new texts, using my own words as using my own words as appropriate. (LIT 3-05a)

| | | | |
|---|---|---|---|

I can **independently** select ideas and relevant information for different purposes, organise essential information or ideas and any **supporting details** in a logical order, and use suitable vocabulary to communicate effectively with my audience. (LIT 3-06a)

| | | | |
|---|---|---|---|

### Understanding, analysing, evaluating

I can show my understanding of what I listen to or watch **by commenting, with evidence, on the content and form of short and extended texts.** (LIT 3-07a)

| | | | |
|---|---|---|---|

To help me develop and informed view, **I am learning about the techniques used to influence opinion and how to assess the value of my sources, and I can recognise persuasion**. (LIT 3-08a)

| | | | |
|---|---|---|---|

### Creating Texts

When listening and talking with others for different purposes, I can: communicate information, ideas or opinions; explain processes, concepts or ideas; **identify issues raised, summarise findings or** draw **conclusions**. (LIT 3-09a)

| | | | |
|---|---|---|---|

**I am developing** confidence **when engaging with others within and beyond my place of learning**. I can communicate in a clear, expressive way and **I am learning to select and organise resources** independently. (LIT 3-10a)

| | | | |
|---|---|---|---|

Notes:

## The Language of Debate: Some Useful Phrases

### Stating an Opinion

- In my opinion...
- I think that...
- I believe that...
- If you want my honest opinion....
- As far as I'm concerned...
- If you ask me...
- It's my feeling that...

### Asking for an Opinion /More Information

- What do you think about...?
- Gary, what's your opinion on...?
- Do you have anything to say about this?
- Do you agree with Gary?
- Sandy, could you explain... in more detail?
- Patrick, could you tell us a bit more about...?

### Expressing Agreement

- I agree with you 100 percent.
- I couldn't agree more.
- You're absolutely right.
- Absolutely!
- Exactly!
- I agree with Bob totally!

- That's exactly how I feel.
- I'm afraid I agree with Gary.
- I have to side with Sandy on this one.
- You have a point there.
- Good point!
- Yes, that's true.

### Expressing Disagreement

- I'm sorry but...
- I'm afraid I disagree.
- I totally disagree.
- I beg to differ.
- That's not always true.
- No, I'm not sure about that.
- I see/take your point but...
- I see/get what you mean but...
- I understand what you're saying but...

### Interruptions

- Can I add something here?
- Is it okay if I jump in for a second?
- Could I make a point?
- Can I put in my two pennies' worth?
- Sorry to interrupt, but... (after accidentally interrupting someone)
- Sorry, go ahead. **OR** Sorry, you were saying...
- You didn't let me finish.

### Building on Others' Contributions

- If I could go back to what Sandy said...
- Going back to Gary's point about...
- As Bob said earlier...
- I'd like to add to what Patrick said about...
- As Sandy mentioned earlier...
- Bob made an interesting point about....

### Settling an Argument

- Let's move on...
- I don't think we're going to agree on this. Perhaps we should move on.
- I think we need to agree to disagree.
- I think we should look at the next point / question...
- Ok. I think it's time to move on.

### Concluding

- In conclusion...
- To sum up...
- To re-cap...
- To summarise...
- Finally...
- I would like to leave you with a final thought...

## Tick *the* Talk

- [ ] speaks clearly and can be heard
- [ ] good pace (not too fast /slow)
- [ ] gives eye contact
- [ ] uses any notes, technology or props effectively
- [ ] confident and enthusiastic
- [ ] good body language
- [ ] makes sense; is easy to follow
- [ ] expresses facts, ideas or arguments clearly
- [ ] backs up ideas/points with reasons/evidence
- [ ] visual aids/slides etc. are useful, well-presented
- [ ] talk suitable for audience
- [ ] talk meets its purpose (e.g. to inform, persuade or entertain)
- [ ] good introduction and conclusion
- [ ] can answer questions effectively
- [ ] thanks the audience

Thank you for that _____ talk!
I didn't know that...
I really liked...
My favourite bit was...
Next time you could...

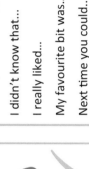

## Tick *the* Talk

- [ ] speaks clearly and can be heard
- [ ] good pace (not too fast/slow)
- [ ] gives eye contact
- [ ] uses any notes, technology or props effectively
- [ ] confident and enthusiastic
- [ ] good body language
- [ ] makes sense; is easy to follow
- [ ] expresses facts, ideas or arguments clearly
- [ ] backs up ideas/points with reasons/evidence
- [ ] visual aids/slides etc. are useful, well-presented
- [ ] talk suitable for audience
- [ ] talk meets its purpose (e.g. to inform, persuade or entertain)
- [ ] good introduction and conclusion
- [ ] can answer questions effectively
- [ ] thanks the audience

Thank you for that _____ talk!
I didn't know that...
I really liked...
My favourite bit was...
Next time you could...

## Tick *the* Talk

- [ ] speaks clearly and can be heard
- [ ] good pace (not too fast/slow)
- [ ] gives eye contact
- [ ] uses any notes, technology or props effectively
- [ ] confident and enthusiastic
- [ ] good body language
- [ ] makes sense; is easy to follow
- [ ] expresses facts, ideas or arguments clearly
- [ ] backs up ideas/points with reasons/evidence
- [ ] visual aids/slides etc. are useful, well-presented
- [ ] talk suitable for audience
- [ ] talk meets its purpose (e.g. to inform, persuade or entertain)
- [ ] good introduction and conclusion
- [ ] can answer questions effectively
- [ ] thanks the audience

Thank you for that _____ talk!
I didn't know that...
I really liked...
My favourite bit was...
Next time you could...

## Tick *the* Talk

- [ ] speaks clearly and can be heard
- [ ] good pace (not too fast /slow)
- [ ] gives eye contact
- [ ] uses any notes, technology or props effectively
- [ ] confident and enthusiastic
- [ ] good body language
- [ ] makes sense; is easy to follow
- [ ] expresses facts, ideas or arguments clearly
- [ ] backs up ideas/points with reasons/evidence
- [ ] visual aids/slides etc. are useful, well-presented
- [ ] talk suitable for audience
- [ ] talk meets its purpose (e.g. to inform, persuade or entertain)
- [ ] good introduction and conclusion
- [ ] can answer questions effectively
- [ ] thanks the audience

Thank you for that _____ talk!
I didn't know that...
I really liked...
My favourite bit was...
Next time you could...

## Tick *the* Talk

- ☐ listens attentively, shows interest; may smile, nod, lean in or have thoughtful/open expression
- ☐ takes turns to talk/listen
- ☐ speaks clearly and can be heard
- ☐ expresses facts, ideas or arguments clearly
- ☐ backs up ideas/points with reasons/evidence
- ☐ uses the 'language of debate'
- ☐ responds well to questions
- ☐ asks appropriate questions
- ☐ can summarise and build on others' contributions
- ☐ able to challenge, disagree or question others' points tactfully
- ☐ engages respectfully with others at all times
- ☐ generally shows confidence and contributes well
- ☐ facilitates discussion: encourages others to talk/expand on answers
- ☐ leads the discussion; keeps group on task; manages difficulties

GROUP ✓

## Tick *the* Talk

- ☐ listens attentively, shows interest; may smile, nod, lean in or have thoughtful/open expression
- ☐ takes turns to talk/listen
- ☐ speaks clearly and can be heard
- ☐ expresses facts, ideas or arguments clearly
- ☐ backs up ideas/points with reasons/evidence
- ☐ uses the 'language of debate'
- ☐ responds well to questions
- ☐ asks appropriate questions
- ☐ can summarise and build on others' contributions
- ☐ able to challenge, disagree or question others' points tactfully
- ☐ engages respectfully with others at all times
- ☐ generally shows confidence and contributes well
- ☐ facilitates discussion: encourages others to talk/expand on answers
- ☐ leads the discussion; keeps group on task; manages difficulties

GROUP ✓

## Tick *the* Talk

- ☐ listens attentively, shows interest; may smile, nod, lean in or have thoughtful/open expression
- ☐ takes turns to talk/listen
- ☐ speaks clearly and can be heard
- ☐ expresses facts, ideas or arguments clearly
- ☐ backs up ideas/points with reasons/evidence
- ☐ uses the 'language of debate'
- ☐ responds well to questions
- ☐ asks appropriate questions
- ☐ can summarise and build on others' contributions
- ☐ able to challenge, disagree or question others' points tactfully
- ☐ engages respectfully with others at all times
- ☐ generally shows confidence and contributes well
- ☐ facilitates discussion: encourages others to talk/expand on answers
- ☐ leads the discussion; keeps group on task; manages difficulties

GROUP ✓

## Tick *the* Talk

- ☐ listens attentively, shows interest; may smile, nod, lean in or have thoughtful/open expression
- ☐ takes turns to talk/listen
- ☐ speaks clearly and can be heard
- ☐ expresses facts, ideas or arguments clearly
- ☐ backs up ideas/points with reasons/evidence
- ☐ uses the 'language of debate'
- ☐ responds well to questions
- ☐ asks appropriate questions
- ☐ can summarise and build on others' contributions
- ☐ able to challenge, disagree or question others' points tactfully
- ☐ engages respectfully with others at all times
- ☐ generally shows confidence and contributes well
- ☐ facilitates discussion: encourages others to talk/expand on answers
- ☐ leads the discussion; keeps group on task; manages difficulties

GROUP ✓

# References and Further Reading

## 1 You Are What You Read

***Curriculum for Excellence*** https://education.gov.scot/

Clark and Rumbold (2006) ***Reading for Pleasure: A Research Overview***, National Literacy Trust
www.literacytrust.org.uk/assets/0000/0562/Reading_pleasure_2006.pdf

***Education Endowment Foundation***
https://educationendowmentfoundation.org.uk/resources/teaching-learning-toolkit/

***Accelerated Reader*** http://readforpleasure.co.uk/

## 2 How to Build a Reader

***The Effects of Synthetic Phonics Teaching on Reading and Spelling Attainment: A Seven Year Longitudinal Study*** by Rhona Johnston and Joyce Watson
www.gov.scot/Resource/Doc/36496/0023582.pdf
www.gov.scot/Resource/Doc/933/0044071.pdf

***Independent Review of the Teaching of Early Reading*** (Final Report 2006) by Sir Jim Rose
http://dera.ioe.ac.uk/5551/2/report.pdf

***Follow-up Study from Reception to Year 1 (2010-2013) and Summary Report of an earlier Longitudinal Study (1997-2004) The Effects of a Systematic, Synthetic Phonics Programme on Reading and Spelling*** by Dr Marlynne Grant
www.syntheticphonics.net/pdf/2014-Report.pdf

Gough & Tunmer (1986) ***Decoding, reading and reading disability:*** Remedial and Special Education, 7, 6-10.

Dr Louisa C. Moats Ed.D. ***Teaching Reading Is Rocket Science What Expert Teachers of Reading Should Know and Be Able To Do***

**Further Reading:**

***Reading by six - how the best schools do it*** (2010) Ofsted
www.gov.uk/government/uploads/system/uploads/attachment_data/file/379093/
Reading_20by_20six.pdf

***Early Reading Instruction: What Science Really Tells Us about How to Teach Reading*** by Diane McGuinness

***Phonics and the Resistance to Reading*** by Mike Lloyd-Jones

***Essential Websites:***

www.phonicsinternational.com : free resources, assessments, plus access to programme and forum
www.debbiehepplewhitehandwriting.com : free handwriting resources and guidance
www.alphabeticcodecharts.com : free alphabetic code charts for different audiences and purposes
www.dyslexics.org.uk : comprehensive site about dyslexia and learning to read, write and spell
www.rrf.org.uk : The Reading Reform Foundation—research, articles and forum
www.iferi.org : International Foundation for Effective Reading Instruction, research and forum
www.thatreadingthing.com: phonics training & reading intervention programme for teens/adults

## 3 Planning, Tracking and Assessment

***Literacy and English Benchmarks*** (Curriculum for Excellence)
https://education.gov.scot/improvement/Documents/LiteracyEnglishBenchmarks.pdf

Topping (2016) ***Theoretical and Empirical Indicators of Implementation Integrity in Book Reading***
http://info.renaissance.com/UK-Impact-Report.html

***Phonics Screening Check Materials***
https://www.gov.uk/government/publications/phonics-screening-check-2017-materials

***Embedding Formative Assessment*** by Dylan Wiliam
***Outstanding Formative Assessment*** by Shirley Clarke

## 4 Teaching and Learning: Short Read

Ellis & Sosu (2014) ***Joseph Rowntree Foundation: Closing the attainment gap in Scottish education***
www.jrf.org.uk/report/closing-attainment-gap-scottish-education

Lunzer & Gardner (1979) ***Effective Use of Reading***
Lunzer & Gardner (1984) ***Learning from the Written Word***

## 5 Teaching and Learning: Long Read

***Read On Get On Scotland*** (Save the Children)
http://www.savethechildren.org.uk/sites/default/files/images/Read_On_Get_On_Scotland.pdf

***Reading Reconsidered: A Practical Guide to Rigorous Literacy Instruction*** by Doug Lemov & C. Driggs

## 6. Managing Reading in the Classroom

***What can parents do to help their children succeed in school?*** (2011) OECD
https://www.oecd.org/pisa/49012097.pdf

***Raising Kids Who Read*** by Daniel T. Willingham
***Growing a Reader from Birth*** by Diane McGuinness

# Useful Websites

*LOOK* Supporting lesson plans, activities, and resources to get you started can be downloaded here—or use the QR code—fancy!

**www.thelearningzoo.co.uk/bookstuff**

## Finding Texts

**http://etc.usf.edu/lit2go**
Classic children's literature to copy and paste; audio tracks for some titles

**www.scran.ac.uk @Scranlife** (log-in required; most local authorities have subscriptions)
**http://simple.wikipedia.org/wiki/Main_Page**
**www.bbc.co.uk/newsround @BBCNewsround**
**www.literacyshed.com @LiteracyShed**

## Read, Listen and Watch: Moving Image Education

**www.bfi.org.uk @BFI**
Download the BFI's Teaching Guide to Film and TV

**http://scottishfilm.education @ScotFilmEd**
**https://movingimageeducation.org @MovingImageEd**

**https://screeningshorts.org.uk/**
Screening Shorts features over 40 licensed films from the world of fiction and visual story-telling for use in the classroom; GLOW log-in required

**http://www.filmeducation.org/resources/ @The_Film_Space**

**http://www.intofilm.org/ @intofilm_edu**
UK wide organisation for film education; born from First Light and Film Club

**http://eightandahalf.org/ @moviebirthday**
The 8½ Foundation is a Scottish-based not-for-profit organisation dedicated to introducing world cinema to children. Its aim is to create a new birthday: a film birthday, at the age of 8½, that celebrates the power of cinema to expand children's horizons

**www.floodfilm.com @TimFloodfilm**
Filmmaker Tim Flood offers CPD and CLPL in film making and using film as text for teachers in Scotland

## Finding Books

**www.clpe.org.uk/corebooks @clpe1**
Comprehensive selection of booklists and high quality texts for children (Ages 3-11)
Free; registration required

**www.booksforkeeps.co.uk @BooksForKeeps**
UK's leading, independent children's book magazine with reviews, articles and interviews with authors and illustrators (free)

**www.worldbookday.com @WorldBookDayUK**
Resources, ideas and activities

**www.thebookpeople.co.uk @TheBookPeople**
Boxed sets to supplement the library or split and give as end of year gifts

**www.lovereading4kids.co.uk @lovereadingkids**
Online independent children's bookstore with reviews and extracts

## Weekly News

Online content and teacher resources available
**www.firstnews.co.uk @FirstNews_Teach**

**www.theweekjunior.co.uk @theweekjunior**

## Essential Subscriptions

Intelligent reading for 7-12 year-olds; science, history and general knowledge
**www.aquila.co.uk @AquilaMag**

Comics and magazines for children
**www.magazine.co.uk/kids-magazines**

## Author Visits and Events

Keep up to date with the Scottish book scene
**www.scottishbooktrust.com @scottishbktrust**

**@BookWeekScot**

## Interactive E-books

For ages 7-12, new chapters released on Fridays
**www.fictionexpress.co.uk @fictionexpress**

## Audio Books

Download to your pc, music player or tablet
**www.audible.co.uk**
and always check www.youtube.com

# Book Suggestions

## For the Teacher's Desk

*Poems to Perform* by Julia Donaldson
*Read me and Laugh: A funny poem for every day of the year* chosen by Gaby Morgan
*The Works: Every Kind of Poem You Will Ever Need at School* by Paul Cookson
*This Little Puffin: A Treasury of Nursery Rhymes, Songs and Games* by Elizabeth Matterson
*A Little, Aloud, for Children* by Michael Morpurgo and Angela Macmillan
*The Puffin Book of Fantastic First Poems* by June Crebbin
*Revolting Rhymes, Dirty Beasts and Rhyme Stew* all by Roald Dahl
*Please Mrs Butler* by Allan Ahlberg
*My Very First Joke Book* by Kaye Umansky
*Roald Dahl's Marvellous Joke Book* by Roald Dahl
*The Little Book of Thunks: 260 questions to make your brain go ouch!* by Ian Gilbert
'Page-a-Day' desk calendar with quotations, new words, jokes or puzzles etc.
'Word of the Day' apps such as 'A Year of Riddles' and 'Vocabulary HD'
*Fink* Question Cards/Conversation Starters

## Books in Scots

### Early/First Level
*The Gruffalo* and *The Gruffalo's Wean* by Julia Donaldson and James Robertson
*A Wee Book o' Fairy Tales in Scots* by Matthew Fitt and James Robertson
*Katie's Pairty* by James Robertson (part of the Katie Series)
*Hamish McHaggis* in English with Scots words and phrases by Linda Strachan

### Second/Third Level
*The Derk Isle* (Adventurs o'Tintin) Hergé and Susan Rennie
*Asterix and the Pechts* by Jean-Yves Ferri and Matthew Fitt
*The Eejits and Geordie's Mingin' Medicine* by Roald Dahl and Matthew Fitt
*The Sleekit Mr Tod* by Roald Dahl and James Robertson
*Precious and the Mischief at Meerkat Brae* by Alexander McCall Smith and James Robertson

See also 'The Kist/A'Chiste' anthology, all schools in Scotland have a copy.

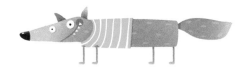

# Permissions: Illustrations & Photos

We would like to thank the following for permission to reproduce illustrations and/or photographs:

Comprehension Compass Design by Katie Quinn Illustration www.oohkatieq.co.uk

Cover image and most illustrations:
© Can Stock Photo / Popmarleo (foxes, animal characters, books and endpapers)
© Can Stock Photo / jrtb: blue post-it note (p3, p51) / mrslevite: cabbages (p142)

© Shutterstock /
Eric Gevaert: Giraffe (Introduction)
Tatiana Bobkova: Girl in a yellow dress reading a book (Chapter 1 introduction, p136)
Subbotina Anna: Two kids using tablet under blanket at night (p17, p136)
Eric Isselee: Ferret sitting, looking at the camera (p29)
Tania Kolinko: Children reading books in classroom (p39, p136)
Martin Kraft: Giraffe isolated on white with shadow (p62)
Rawpixel.com: Father and daughter reading (p63, p134)
Monkey Business Images: Children reading books in classroom (p123)
Tomsickova Tatyana: Boy, sitting in a book store, reading books (p134, p149)
Yuliya Evstratenko: Little girl reading a book with her dog in the outdoors (p97)
DoubleBubble: black and white pig (p88)
Khabarushka: pug (Dug the Plenary Pug) (p6, p128, p144)
Gresei: chocolate bar (p68, p85, p86)
Farianna: Vintage Glasses with chain (p12)
Aksenova Natalya: Seashell on white background (p14)
Alis Photo: wooden retro car toy (p11)
Andrea Slatter: Red headed boy wearing blue striped shirt (p125)
Richard Peterson: bucket of chicken (p69)

Mini Me Sticks at West Linton Primary School (p20)
Richard Lammerts: Dreamstime; Elephant with long trunk (p89)
Monopoly Arrow : Jbarta (Public Domain) via Wikimedia Commons (p106/various)
Bardon Infants' School, Infants' Class, Reading (April 1951) Queensland State Archives, Digital Image ID 1629 (Public Domain) (p126)
Anne and children at Edinburgh Academy Junior School (p156)
Tommy Thumb's Pretty Song Book (1744) (Public Domain) John Newbury (1713–1767)
Beatrix Potter, Aleph-bet Books, (Public Domain) (p80)
Roald Dahl (l) en Nannie Kuiper 13 oktober 1982, Author © Hans van Dijk / Anefo licensed under the Creative Commons Attribution-Share Alike 3.0 Unported license (p85/86)
Bloom's Taxonomy by Xristina la (Own work) [CC BY-SA 3.0 (http://creativecommons.org/licenses/by-sa/3.0)], via Wikimedia Commons (p100)

All other images used are in the public domain and do not require any citation.

# Permissions

We would like to gratefully acknowledge and thank the publishers and authors for permission to reproduce the following copyright material:

Extracts from **Curriculum for Excellence**, the **Experiences and Outcomes** and the **Literacy and English Principles and Practice** © Crown Copyright 2017
Reproduced under the terms of the Open Government Licence
http://www.nationalarchives.gov.uk/doc/open-government-licence/version/3/

**Nostalgia as Pebbledash** by Jonny Walker (p11-14)
From *The Feeling of Reading*
Reproduced with permission of the author

**For my Grandmother Knitting** by Liz Lochhead (p121)
From *A Choosing: Selected Poems* (Polygon 2011)
Reproduced with permission of Birlinn through PLSclear

**The English Alphabetic Code** (p33-p34) © Phonics International and © Debbie Hepplewhite
Reproduced with permission of the author

**Questions Prompts for Moving Image Texts** (p117)
Adapted from *The Three Cs and The Three Cs* by Tim Flood
http://www.floodfilm.com/literacy/3cs-and-3ss/ Tim Flood
Reproduced with permission of the author

**World Book Day: quarter of children would not own a book without it** (p120)
Published March 1, 2017 by Heloise Wood
Text adapted from http://www.thebookseller.com/news/one-four-childrens-first-book-bought-wbd-token-499621 Reproduced with permission of *The Bookseller*

**It's time to reclaim world book day by DADDACOOL** (p119)
Text adapted from http://www.daddacool.co.uk/2017/02/time-reclaim-world-book-day.html
Reproduced with permission of the author, Alex Walsh

**Bees' Wings and Spiders' Ankles** by Anne Glennie (p148)

Every effort has been made to trace copyright holders of material reproduced in this book, and the publishers apologise for any inadvertent omissions.

# Acknowledgements

I would like to thank teachers and schools across Scotland for their support with my work, especially all of the anonymous teachers who spend time making and sharing resources for the *Teaching Trunk* on the *Learning Zoo* website for colleagues everywhere; you are saving so many Sunday nights.

Special thanks to children, teachers and all staff at the following schools for their help and contributions to *Reflective Reading*. A huge thank you also to Janey Ross (and her Primary 2 class!) for writing such a clear and comprehensive case study for this book.

Dean Park Primary School, Edinburgh
Edinburgh Academy Junior School, Edinburgh
Riverside Primary School, Stirling
St Andrew's Fox Covert RC Primary School, Edinburgh
St Columba's Primary School, Oban
Tolsta Primary School, Isle of Lewis
West Linton Primary School, Scottish Borders

Thank you to colleagues and friends in the RRF (The Reading Reform Foundation) and IFERI (International Foundation for Effective Reading Instruction) whose knowledge, work and experience in the field of phonics continues to inform my work. Special thanks to Debbie Hepplewhite, Susan Godsland and Dr Marlynne Grant for their support, mentorship and friendship.

Thank you to all of my teachers at Mount Carmel and Stewarton Academy, and to those who encouraged me in education; your belief in me made a difference: Mrs Clarke, Ros. Wilson, Lorna Walter and Diana Mackinnon.

Thank you is not enough for my friend, Zoo colleague, and editor for this title, Helen MacKinven. For keeping me and my teacher-tone in check, and for support in everything—thank you, Buddy.

For my family, for their unfailing support—and suffering—through all of my mad-cap adventures, from moving to an island and breeding alpacas to starting three businesses in three years and writing this book.

For Lauren, who loved *Nandy's Bedtime* for the longest time and Harris, who claims he learned everything he knows from television (especially the big words) xx

For Iain. For everything. Thank you x

# About the Author

Anne Glennie is a literacy consultant, author and trainer. Her current courses include *Reflective Reading* and *Phonics Forever*. To date, she has trained over 10,000 teachers in all aspects of literacy across Scotland. A classroom teacher first and foremost, Anne provides training that delegates describe as 'creative', 'fun' and 'inspirational'—with an emphasis on the practicalities of teaching and learning in the primary classroom.

With a degree in English Language and Literature, Anne has always been passionate about learning and books, and she is now a publisher at Cranachan Publishing, specialising in high quality, Scottish historical fiction for children and teaching resources for schools. She has also written several (phonically decodable) reading books for a leading educational publisher's reading scheme.

Anne is a founding committee member of IFERI—the International Foundation for Effective Reading Instruction, a member of the RRF (The Reading Reform Foundation) and is known for her thought-provoking education comment pieces.

When Anne is not training or travelling, she can be found in the remote wilds of Scotland where she lives on the edge of the Atlantic on the Isle of Lewis, with her husband, two children, ten Hebridean sheep and one Moomin (French Bulldog). She collects vintage Ladybird books and she shares her office with a giant stuffed giraffe called Jeffrey.

**@anneglennie**    #staycurious

## Further Information

To find out more about training options, or to read Anne's blog, visit:
**www.thelearningzoo.co.uk**

To connect with Anne directly you can tweet her **@anneglennie** or you can email her **anne@thelearningzoo.co.uk**

Find out more about her books for schools and her publishing venture here:
**www.cranachanpublishing.co.uk** and follow **@cranachanbooks** on Twitter.